SEARCHING
FOR
JOHN BALL

A Father and Daughter's Inspiring Journey
Researching the Life and Letters
Of a Civil War Ancestor

By Cynthia B. Hanson

With research assistance from Eugene Ross Hanson
And a foreword by Wayne Jorgenson

Galloping Hills
PUBLISHING

1st Edition Printing, May 2013
ISBN: 978-0-615-68010-1
Printed in the USA

Cover design by Hari Krishnan, *plananddesignsite.com*
Cover photo of John Ball courtesy Wayne Jorgenson
Cover and back cover background image courtesy the Library of Congress,
Prints & Photographs Division, Civil War Photographs,
[Digital ID cph.3b41990]

To my children—
Sturdy shoots spring from strong roots.

*"Every man realized in an instant what that order meant –
death or wounds to us all, the sacrifice of a regiment to gain a few
minutes time."*

Lieutenant William Lochren,
First Minnesota Volunteer Infantry

Acknowledgments

I wish to thank the men of the First Minnesota Regiment for their bravery and staggering sacrifice of life on the battlefield of Gettysburg. Many historians have referred to their courageous act of marching into a bloodbath with the first oncoming Confederates as a sacrifice integral to turning the Civil War.

I'm grateful to the many people who offered advice, encouragement, and time during the research and writing of this book: my father, Eugene Ross Hanson, for his help, untiring support, and unwavering trust that I would follow through with this project despite its many challenges; my husband, Jeff Richards, for his patience and encouragement; Wayne Jorgenson, historian and owner of the largest private collection of First Minnesota artifacts; Archivist Patrick Bowmaster, who acted as a guidepost for the transcriptions and historical accuracy; Genealogist Diana Horning, who added intrigue and valuable information; Francis Jackson (husband of Johan Ball), Martha West, and Edith Bartley for their research and contributions to the Ball genealogy; school principal and history buff M. P. Stone, for her research and generous time photographing the Ball structures in New York; The Minnesota Historical Society, for permission to quote from "No More Gallant a Deed;" the Winona Historical Society, for their gracious acceptance of and care for the letters in their archives; contributors to the Winona Newspaper Project for countless hours spent creating a historic newspaper database; filmmaker David Padrusch, for his interest and collaborative efforts; Emma Lewton Ball, John's wife, and his daughter, Mary, for preserving the letters; John Ball, a remarkable man and great-great grandfather to whom I grew very close while documenting his life. His accomplishments in his short span of 39 years were extraordinary.

"Of ... John Ball, too much cannot be said in his praise. He participated in the first battle at Bull Run, where he displayed much sagacity and courage. From this time his regiment seemed destined to be foremost in all the battles of the Army of the Potomac. He was at Yorktown and Williamsburg, and in the memorable six days' fight on the banks of Fredericksburg under General Burnside, and in the hottest of the fight at the battle of Chancellorsville under Hooker, and at Gettysburg. In the latter engagement all the superior officers of his brigade were killed or wounded, and the formation of the brigade devolved upon him. The part he took on that bloody field will never be released from the pages of history. After the disbandment of his regiment he was appointed colonel of the 11th Minnesota, with which he remained until the close of the war. Col. Ball was wounded at Bristow Station by a ball passing through his thigh. He had fired every charge of his ammunition, and being almost hand to hand with the enemy, he threw his pistol at them, and the next moment received a disabling wound. He returned to Minnesota after the close of the war, where he married Emma C. Lewton, of Winona, Minn. He died of consumption at the home of his parents, in this town, September 26, 1875."

—Child's Gazetteer of Jefferson County,
Town of Rutland, 1890

Foreword

History has a fascination for many people because it speaks to our roots and to who we are as a people. When one thinks of the pivotal events in American history, one that must be considered is the American Civil War. The pivotal battle of the Civil War was the Battle of Gettysburg, fought over a three day period from July 1 to July 3, 1863. During that battle, many regiments played important roles; one of the foremost was the First Minnesota Infantry. Drill down further to see what officers led these men so well during the war, and one of the names that arises is that of John Ball.

When Capt. John McCallum was wounded at the Battle of Fredericksburg, 1st Lt. Ball took command of Company F. He led them at Gettysburg and was promoted to the rank of captain shortly after the battle. Ball was seriously wounded at the Battle of Bristoe Station, but he survived and was with the regiment when they were discharged on May 5, 1864. Governor Steven Miller, who also served in the First Minnesota, recognized Ball's value and gave the valiant officer a commission to serve as the lieutenant colonel in command of the 11th Minnesota Infantry. Ball then reentered the service on Sept 10, 1864, and served until the end of the war, being discharged on June 26, 1865. He rose through the ranks, from 1st sergeant to lieutenant colonel in command, and participated in 22 battles during his service.

While John Ball was not an exceptional writer, his letters are important because they tell us something about the man and in turn about the regiment. Through them we are educated about the hardships, concerns, hopes, and dreams as well as the monotony of daily life.

These letters are a source of civic pride in Winona, Minn., where he served as a surveyor, town treasurer, and state legislator. It was in Winona that he raised his family prior to his death in 1875 at the age of only 39. The letters are now in the care of the Winona County Historical Society for future generations to research and enjoy.

In "Searching for John Ball," Ms. Hanson includes how she and her father went about gathering information on their ancestor, transcribing letters, and talking with Civil War historians to gain insight into the life of the Civil War soldier and the meaning behind some of the terms he used, thus bringing more clarity and life to the letters he wrote. Part of the book's intent is to inspire others to dig into those "old letters" stored in the closet somewhere and preserve their ancestors' stories, who paved the way for them so many years ago. The book includes an afterword on how to research an ancestor.

Ms. Hanson has included the story so many people wish they could experience—the journey of family discovery. Some letters were found, and thus began a search of curiosity that led to the Civil War and a courageous officer who wrote them. As their research developed, both Cynthia and her father realized the importance of preserving his letters for historic perpetuity and for family genealogic research. But they also felt compelled to "immortalize" an ancestor whose historic contributions deserved to be recorded before the letters faded into obscurity.

The story of the First Minnesota and the story of John Ball is one of honor. Sit back and enjoy learning about a regiment through the eyes of one man, and the search for the details of his life that stitched his story together.

Wayne Jorgenson is the author of "Every Man Did His Duty," distributed by Tesora Books, and co-creator of the website www.1stminnesota.net.

Courtesy of Winnona County Historical Society Archives

A Noteworthy Life

I was visiting my father in Vermont in the year 2000 when our conversation drifted to the Civil War. Eventually he rose from his chair, left the room, and returned with a packet of tattered, yellowed letters secured with a single leather cord. We untied the bow that bound together this collection of his great grandfather's Civil War correspondence and gingerly unfolding one of the fragile documents in search of a letter that referenced Major General Joseph Hooker. At that moment, it occurred to us that the time had come to transcribe these historic accounts for perpetuity.

Our ancestor, John Ball, was one of the first to enlist as a private in the Union forces in 1861. He fought in most of the major battles, including Gettysburg, and survived a near-fatal wound at the Battle of Bristoe Station. He was promoted to lieutenant colonel to command the 11th Minnesota Volunteer Infantry in Gallatin, Tenn., in a reconstruction effort after the war.

The nearly 70 letters that span from 1861 to 1875, plus certificates, supply lists, a Brooks Brothers bill, and other war documents, were shuttled from desks to dresser drawers to attics by three generations. They were in remarkably good condition considering their age. My father had intended to transcribe the packet and incorporate them into a thesis at Yale University, but his life took a different turn, and the letters sat in an

1

attic until they were unearthed. As we glanced through the aging packet, we realized that if someone didn't transcribe them soon, a valuable historic contribution could be lost for future generations.

Thus began a dedicated search that included visits to archivists, travels to upstate New York, and late-night sessions that sometimes involved deciphering fading penmanship inscribed in centuries-old pencil. John illegibly scribbled some of the letters while propped up on a knee as he lay on the floor of his tent. In those midnight sessions, I began to wonder if my great-great grandfather could have ever imagined his great-great granddaughter sitting at an electric machine meticulously transcribing his correspondence while munching on Kit Kat bars.

Then a bit of a mystery unfolded: Among the historic references was a notation about John's adoption shortly after his birth. Surprised by my findings, I contacted three genealogists in the Rutland, New York, area where he grew up to determine if we could learn more about his parentage and heritage. Two genealogists were unavailable to work on the project, but a third responded to my initial query with great interest.

"You intrigued me right away because I, too, was born in the town of Rutland; there's a good chance that I would have already heard of your gr.-gr.-grandfather, and possibly have done some research on his line, but since you didn't include his name, I'll have to wait to find out," wrote Diana Horning.

I replied with basic information about my research and received the following response: "I was very surprised to hear that you are researching the name Ball because I now live with my mother in the house built by William P. Ball in the mid-1800s. I have not researched the Ball family but am interested to know if he is related to your John Ball. We refer to William as "Grandpa Ball" even though we aren't related as far as we know; one reason for that is probably that my parents knew his descendants, the Johnsons. That was a while ago—my Mom's now 90 yrs. old. I barely remember seeing Roy Johnson when I was a kid."

"Yes, our John Ball was the son of William Pelton Ball!" I replied in amazement. "And his sister, Agnes, married Mr. Johnson."

A remarkable exchange ensued in which Ms. Horning divulged that her family was convinced of a sad presence inhabiting their house. Several family members claimed to have felt that presence in what was said to have been John's bedroom. I was so astonished by her response that I cut off our communication, thinking that it was too much of a coincidence that on my first attempt to find a historical researcher, I had connected with one who actually lived in John's childhood home.

A year later I contacted a history buff through the Rutland Town Hall—a school principal who offered to take photographs of the houses and barns owned by the Ball family. I asked M. P. Stone if she could research the ownership of William Ball's house. A week later she wrote the following response about some photographs, including the William Ball house, that she sent: "The last 3 (white house) are of the W. P. Ball house ... mail and the paper are still being delivered so it must be inhabited. W. P. Ball House history so far: Kerber, Dathan R. and Horning, Diana L. own it.... The deed was passed on in 1999."

Diana Horning did, indeed, own John's childhood home! Thus began our search for John Ball, a path that took me and my 79-year-old father to Rutland and Watertown, N.Y., where we visited courthouses, libraries, and John's homestead with hopes of uncovering any information about him, including his blood parentage. The only clue we had to his actual heritage was a sentence he penned to his parents on April 16th, 1862, during his internment at the Fortress Monroe Hospital recovering from what was believed to be bronchitis but more likely were the early stages of tuberculosis: "Well I hope as a regular Irishman would that because I am writing from a hospital you will not think that I am killed or mortally wounded."

John must have known he was adopted because references to it appeared in the 1850 Rutland census when he was 15. He may have known who his blood parents were. Did he also know that he possibly was of Irish descent?

We searched reference books in the Flower Memorial Library genealogy room in Watertown and visited the courthouse in search of adoption records. We met Ms. Horning and her mother and visited the white, clapboard farmhouse surrounded by farmer's fields where he grew up. Jars of newly canned fruits and vegetables lined the kitchen counter; the interior seemed in keeping with the original late 1880s style. We climbed the stairs to view the small room with slanted ceilings where John likely succumbed to tuberculosis at the age of 39. He left his wife and three children behind in Minnesota in 1875 to journey back on the train to the Rutland home for those final days. Ms. Horning's 90-year-old mother sat quietly in the kitchen while we plied her with questions about the house and neighboring Johnson family, who John's sister married into. Ball family members had taken turns living in the house well into the 1900s.

Our search took a new turn with the introduction of Patrick Bowmaster, archivist at the Mary Baker Eddy Library at the First Church of Christ Scientist in Boston. Fastidious and thoughtful, Mr. Bowmaster had a personal interest and educational background in Civil War history. He spent a considerable amount of time helping with background research and instructing on the proper methodology for transcribing historic documents. We used the large magnifier to decipher some of the letters' more illegible handwriting, which belonged to many different hands as John had saved correspondence from his family, friends, military personnel, merchants, and others.

Transcribing old letters is fraught with challenges: We did the best we could, but many were too faded or torn to be able to decipher the original message. Therefore, the reader of this book needs to recognize that our limited capabilities left much unanswered in the transcriptions; the letters in this book are not a complete reflection of the originals. Brackets and notations were needed by the transcriber to explain missing content. Additionally, the language of the time was different than it is today. For example, an "ff" at the end of a word was replaced by the ending of "s" over time. Historical linguistics was honored in the transcribing, and spelling and grammatical errors were left in the transcriptions to maintain the most accurate record possible with the limited resources at hand.

The book is structured in a way in which the letters are interwoven into the various years and stages of John's life instead of compiled sequentially at the end of the book. This allows the reader to review relevant letters relating to specific events in John's life within the same section. For example, letters relating to the Battle of Gettysburg are included in the chapter "Sacrifices at Gettysburg and Bristoe Station."

Worth noting is that there are more letters written by John to fellow soldiers and family members that are missing from the packet. One missing letter was written to his parents from the Battlefield of Gettysburg.

The search for John Ball sparked a friendship with Wayne Jorgenson, an avid Civil War historian and collector of First Minnesota memorabilia who lives in Minnesota. Mr. Jorgenson has meticulously documented information on John's regiment, and his website includes extensive information about First Minnesota soldiers, battles, photographs, and other factual information. He is to be commended for his preservation of facts, documents, clothing, letters, personal details, and books relating to one of the most noteworthy regiments of the Civil War.

The search also prompted a trip to the Gettysburg Memorial—an austere park where a solemn hush seems to sweep through the vast stretch of monuments. I hiked up Little Round Top and then visited the First Minnesota monument. The field beyond the monument where thousands of soldiers were left partially buried after Pickett's Charge is particularly striking when one knows that the First Minnesota Regiment incurred one of the greatest losses in military history on July 2, 1863—some 82 percent. Of the 242 men ordered to charge the 1,600 oncoming Alabama rebels, only 47 survived. Yet despite the extreme odds against them, in the end their flag was still aloft. The memorial plaque next to the First Minnesota monument documents their experience:

> *"Late on the afternoon of July 2, after the collapse of the Union line at the Peach Orchard, Confederate infantry in front of you threatened to pour through a gap in the Union line here. When Maj. Gen. Winfield S. Hancock, commander of the Union Second Corps, rode up to assess the situation, only one regiment was at hand to stop the Confederate tide—the 1st Minnesota.*
>
> *"My God, are these all the men we have here?" Hancock asked. It was, but they would have to do. "Charge those lines!" shouted Hancock, and immediately the lone regiment swept down the slope "double quick." With leveled bayonets, the Minnesotans crashed into Brig. Gen. Cadmus M. Wilcox's Alabamians who outnumbered them 4-to-1.*
>
> *The charge broke the Confederate ranks and stalled the Southerners long enough for Union reinforcements, but at a terrific cost. According to a regimental officer, of the 262 Minnesotans in the charge, only 47 escaped death or injury."*

The search for John Ball resulted in a common purpose that bound my father and me in ways we had never experienced: a sense of responsibility to transcribe a historic packet of letters, document our relative's significant life, and donate the packet to a historical society to add to our nation's collective understanding of the Civil War. We made the long trek to Winona, Minn., from our respective homes and donated the letters at a ceremony at the Winona Historical Society on Oct. 17, 2012, to honor John Ball's contributions to his town, state, and country—and his remarkable leadership role and survival in the battle of Gettysburg.

> At Gettysburg his regiment suffered severely, eight times the colors were shot down, but each time they came up again and were brought safely off the field. The commissioned officers were all killed or disabled except two, Capt. Ball being one of the two, the command of the little remnant of the brave old regiment devolving on him for a short time.
>
> —Jefferson County Journal, Sept. 29, 1875

Researching the life of John Ball also served to bond me to a great-great grandfather who left behind a few photographs and a record of his Civil War experience. In his relatively short span on earth, he played a significant role fighting 22 battles in the Civil War, helping to turn the war at Gettysburg, and aiding in reconciling the North and South in Gallatin, Tenn. For that he deserves recognition for contributions that helped to shape American history.

John Ball at age 12.

The Early Years in Rutland

Shortly after they were married in 1834, William Pelton Ball and Adelia Arodyne Hill Ball adopted a newborn baby, according to "Child's Gazetteer of Jefferson County—Town of Rutland." It's unlikely the infant was adopted as a farm hand, as was customarily done during that era, since most worker children were brought onto farms at older ages when they could be of greater use milking the cows and sowing seeds in the fields. Nor was it likely that John was taken into their home because Adelia was believed to be barren, since the couple had been married only a little over a year.

One likely scenario is that John, who was adopted as a newborn shortly after his birth date of Dec. 5, 1835, had a mother who died in childbirth. This is a good possibility because statistics from the mid-1800's show that about one of every seven women died in childbirth, and it was even more likely if the mother had twins. There are no records of any female Ball or Hill family members dying around the time of his birth, but the Hill genealogy is incomplete in terms of death notices. Another possibility is that he was the son of a cook, housekeeper, or farm hand in the Ball household who was unable to care for him.

John's adoption was unusual in the 1830s. Guardianships were more common. Adoption was not recognized in the United States until Massachusetts enacted the first statute in 1851, yet the 1850 Rutland census shows him as adopted. A trip to the Watertown probate court in search of John's parentage served fruitless: New York has strict laws regarding access to adoption records. Additionally, there were few or no records early enough to date back to John's birth, according to the court.

Another possibility is that John was born out of wedlock to an aunt, of which there were 12 between the 2 families. Adelia Arodyne Hill Ball, John's mother, was the daughter of Asa and Katherine Hill, who moved to Rodman, N.Y., from Holliston, Mass., in 1810. According to genealogical records, the Hills had three sons and seven daughters, although birth and death records exist for only five of the daughters.

In the 1850 census for Rodman, Talcott (age 35) and Sophronia Hill Merwin (age 31) were living with Charles Hill, age 15. Charles was described as a laborer attending school. The Merwins had no children and were "loyal members and active workers of the Sunday School, he teaching the adult men's class and she the primary boy's class," according to genealogy records. There is no record of any Hill siblings having a son named Charles. There are no census records showing that he was adopted by the Merwins.

Charles Hill and John Ball were similar ages—records show them both as born "about 1835" or "about 1836." They may have been twins from a mother who died in childbirth, was overwhelmed with caring for both at once, or had an out-of-wedlock birth.

The 1850 census also shows Asa (age 78) and Katherine (age 70) Hill living next door to the Merwins in the home of daughter Mary and Herman Parmale and their three children. Mary died in 1852, and the 1860 census shows the youngest Parmale child (age 14) living with the Merwins, who by then had moved to Rutland. Charles Hill had moved out.

Sometime in the 1860s, Sophronia Hill Merwin's sister, Jenette, moved in with the Merwins. The 1870 and 1880 censuses describe her as an unmarried "tailoress" born in 1815—she was about 20 at the time of John and Charles' births. Jenette could have been John and/or Charles' mother.

"Bear in mind that in 1835, there were NO decent avenues for a woman to make her own living, and certainly not enough to maintain a household. Friends, family, or neighbors might adopt the child" if born out of wedlock, wrote Nan Dixon, coordinator of the Jefferson County historical research facility in Watertown, New York. "In my own family, my great-great grandmother was widowed as a young woman, and bound out (apprenticed) her young son, but was able to keep her daughter until she remarried, which was soon. Adoption and apprenticing were matters of economic necessity."

John appears to have had a strong relationship with his adoptive parents. He was not treated like a farm hand. Writing to him in 1869 about his daughter, Mary, when he was in his 30s, John's mother fondly recollects how she would place him on her lap when he was a child and teach him poetry: "She learn to recite poetry as readily as you used to when I held you in my lap and spun linen," she writes in one letter.

John sometimes signed his letters to his parents with the word "affectionately," and after the Battle of Gettysburg, his father wrote an endearing letter that reflected the proud way he viewed his son:

> "...you better believe there was a rejoicing when we got your letter relieving us of the anxiety and suspense, we was in for a few days for everyone I met the first word was "Have you got a letter from John? Have you heard from ...?" I saw Uncle Samuel Payne. He had read the same in the paper that we had but he said he would bet you would come out all right, said you had been through so many battles and came through all sound—would this time. I saw Orvin Hill just after I got the letter. Told him you was all right. He gave one of his funny laughs. Said he guess you are bullet proof. He had read the same in the paper and thought your chance was small to come out sound."

William Ball, John's father, was well-liked and respected in the community. His obituary noted when he died at age 91, two years after his wife, that he was "widely known and it can be truthfully said that no man in Jefferson county possessed a larger number of friends or fewer enemies than Mr. Ball."

Other newspapers described him as "highly esteemed for his many sterling qualities and ... repeatedly honored by his townsmen by election to the offices of assessor and highway commissioner, holding the latter office for 12 years. For several years he was director of the Agricultural Insurance Co."

> "[William] Ball's ancestors were among the pioneers of Jefferson county, and he was born Nov. 24, 1810, in a log house built by his father when the town was first settled. His parents were Elihu and Anna Pelton Ball, and his grandfather, Nehemiah Ball, was 1st sergeant of an artillery company in 1789. At the age of 24 Mr. Ball married Miss Adelia D. Hill, a daughter of Asa Hill of Rodman, and in the spring of 1825 he bought a farm in the town of Rodman, where he and his wife reared a family of three children, John, an adopted son, Antoinette (Mrs. George F. Hickox) and Agnes O. (Mrs. O. A. Johnson)."
>
> —Watertown Times, April 11, 1902

John's grandfather, Elihu Ball, was described as "industrious" in the "Genealogical and Family History of the County of Jefferson, New York, Vol. 1," having cleared and improved 105 acres of land and built a house and barn within four years. He served in the War of 1812. "Utica was their nearest market; and when their first child was but a year old Mr. and Mrs. Ball went thither on an ox-sled with a barrel of potash, a distance of about 75 miles," according to "Child's Gazetteer."

John probably received a good elementary and secondary education since his grandfather was superintendent of schools for the town of Rutland. A Minnesota newspaper account indicates that he attended Harvard College sometime between 1850 and 1852 (between the ages of 15 and 17), but left college to head west due to health problems. He studied law with the firm of Lewis & Simpson in Winona. Although he was admitted to the bar in 1860, he never practiced law, but it was a useful background to have for surveying and politics, which he pursued in later years.

One can learn a lot about a soldier's educational level by the quality of their handwriting, and John's handwriting was "quite good," according to historical archivist Patrick Bowmaster. The content of his letters are cultivated and insightful. They indicate a keen interest in military strategy and philosophical and religious reflection.

John was the eldest in the family, followed by his sister, Antoinette, and young Agnes. He clearly had a good relationship with his youngest sister, who was nearly 20 years his junior. Among the collection is a sweet letter written in 1863 by Agnes to John when she was 12 where she pens about churning butter and carriage rides with her teacher. When he writes of young Agnes, it's with poetic inferences:

> "I do not know what to say to or of Agnes. I cannot tell how to adress her. I look at her as I have looked at the pelican on the placid lakes of Minnesota. The reflections of their white bodies upon the smooth water with so large and pearly white in the slight angle of incidence and reflection that I could not tell how much of the bird was above the water and how much beneath or which was bird and which was shadow. So I view the growing mind and opening faculties of that sister Agnes on the smooth waters where I at present see her. My allowance for her growth and progress which the change of years must have brought no reflection or image to my mind of the proportions of her soul or intellect. Well I cannot really tell you how much is in the image and how much of the bird is above the water. So although I believe I ought to know my sister, I cannot feel that I know Agnes."

Antoinette was two year younger than John, and there is not a single letter from her in the packet. Despite requests to his parents that she please write him, Antoinette rebuffed his wishes. It appears she also failed to visit him when he returned to Rutland at the age of 39 to die in the family home. There was a clear, unexplained schism between the two siblings. He laments this fact in his lengthy, 21-page letter to his parents from Fortress Monroe Hospital:

> "I owe a Thousand Appologies to Antoinette[.] I shall not censure her a particle if she should discard me as an inconstant brother and undeserving of further attention[.] She has, I confess, much reason to think if I was an

uncharitable and ungrateful Boy. I am unnaturaly indif-
erant to a sisters kindness as a man[.] Please give her my
love and also George (if he is a man who loves his whole
country to well to have it torn assunder). Kiss Willie and
tell him about his <u>mithical</u> uncle John. I say <u>mithical</u> be-
cause he never has [unclear] may see me."

The tension between John and Antoinette perhaps offer a clue as to why John left home in his teens, moving many states west to become a surveyor in Minnesota.

14

Courtesy of Minnesota Historical Society

Early Enlistment in the Infantry

M

The 1850 Rutland, NY, census shows John at age 14 living at home with his family. Three years later, he moves to Minnesota. He arrived in Winona several years later in the company of B. J. Grimshaw, according to "Portrait and Biographical Record of Winona County, Minnesota," published in 1895. He worked for Thomas Simpson, who was surveying the Menomonee Indian Reservation in Wisconsin. Around the age of 17, John Ball somehow became United States Deputy Surveyor, according to Minnesota state records.

The Dec. 26, 1861 St. Cloud Democrat offers clues as to where he might have received his training, which would have taken place around the age of 16: "He spent some time in Harvard College, but his health failing, he came to Minnesota, and was engaged several years in Government surveying, becoming remarkably strong and muscular."

He surveyed tracks of Eastern Sioux Indian territory and created the first plat for the frontier town of Montezuma, Minn., at age 17 on June 19, 1852. Montezuma was renamed Winona in 1853, and it eventually became his future family's hometown, according to the "History of Wabasha County," published in 1884.

"This original plat was bounded on the north by the Mississippi river, on the east by Market street, on the south by Wabasha street, and on the west by Washington street." It comprised a square, each side of which was six full blocks. This plat was enlarged from time to time by 'additions,' until at the close of 1856 the platted area on Wabasha prairie covered a tract of ground fully two miles in extent from east to west and nearly half that distance from north to south."

Winona means "first-born daughter," and the town was named after the Dakota Indian princess We-Noh-Nah, daughter of Chief Wapasha III. It was incorporated in 1855, eventually becoming the third largest city in Minnesota until it was surpassed in the late 1880s and began to dwindle in population at the turn of the century.

John apparently went to Dubuque, Iowa, in the fall of 1855 and returned to Winona the following year as a government surveyor. Land claims became legal in 1855 with the opening of a federal land office. Winona was on the Mississippi River and became a main rail line and shipping port for the burgeoning wheat and lumber trades—over 1,300 steamboats stopping there annually by 1856.

In the 1860 Federal Census for the City of Winona, John Ball was referred to as a 23-year-old white male attorney-at-law, however, he never actually practiced law. He owned an abstract company in town, studied law with the firm of Lewis & Simpson, and was admitted to the Bar in 1860.

On April 29, 1861, at Ft. Snelling near Minneapolis, John was one of the first Union soldiers mustered in. He became an orderly sergeant with the 1st Minnesota Regiment Co. K, which was comprised of 76 men. Most of the men in his company were from Winona, and it was the first regiment offered to President Lincoln after Fort Sumter.

In a firsthand account, Sergeant James A. Wright described the day of enlistment in his memoir "No More Gallant a Deed: A Civil War Memoir of the First Minnesota Volunteers:"

"Before noon the companies from St. Paul, St. Anthony, and Minnesota came in with flags and bands. A garrison flag, rope for the halyards, and ammunition for the cannon also came. ... It was on this occasion—at the close of the cheering—that some of the boys gave the best imitation that they could of an Indian war-whoop, and it became thereafter a distinctive part of the regimental cheering."

Willis A. Gorman, an ex-governor, lawyer, and Democrat in the House of Representatives, was appointed colonel of the regiment; Stephen Miller, a future governor, was appointed lieutenant colonel.

On May 5, Colonel Gorman received orders from Washington to detail two companies and detach them without delay. Once the troops arrived at camp, Sergeant Ball was designated "Mother" as he distributed supplies to the soldiers.

The First Minnesota served in almost every major battle fought by the Army of the Potomac, including Antietam—which has been called the bloodiest day in US history. It claimed more than 23,000 lives and led to Lincoln's issuance of the Emancipation Proclamation, according the National Park Service. In addition to their astronomical losses at Gettysburg, the First Minnesota was the last to leave the battlefield and suffered the highest loss of men of any Federal regiment at the First Battle of Bull Run in 1861—48 killed, 83 wounded, 23 wounded and missing, and 30 missing.

Of the First Battle of Bull Run on July 21, 1861, Sergeant John Merritt, who was awarded the Medal of Honor for taking the rebel flag, left the following account of John Ball's service: "John Ball, the orderly sergeant of K Co., was sick and I was acting orderly sergeant. As sick as Ball was, he came onto the field, and I saw him standing near the regiment while we were engaged, with his arms folded, apparently the most unconcerned person of the lot; he was a brave and fearless man."

But in the only 1861 letter in the collection, written to his parents shortly after the First Battle of Bull Run, John portrays a different image—a man unnerved by his "Bitter" first encounters with the enemy, so much so that he reminds his parents of his Last Will and Testament. It was his first fierce battle, and he was shaken by what he observed.

"Knowing I should soon see the dreaded sight and experience the dangers of a heavy Battle I thought it a

matter of justice to inform you of so much that if I was not permitted to address you again you could presume upon my probable fate and also to speak of those subjects which belonged to you to know concerning my peculiary matters and The Last Will & Testament which I transmitted to you from Fort Snelling."

John wrote a sizable number of letters in the collection to his parents, and in particular, to his father. Many begin formally and apologetically for not having written sooner. The large gaps in time between his correspondences most likely are due to letters missing from the collection or challenging circumstances that made communications nearly impossible, as he points out in several letters to his parents in 1862.

The mail was not reliable, and it took weeks and sometimes months to reach its destination. In an 1863 letter written by soldier Milton Bevans to John Ball, who was now a captain, Bevans laments that his mail was thrown away by a careless sergeant. The fact that Bevans took the time to write an imploring letter to his captain shows just how much the soldiers valued their correspondence during a time when instant communication was a pipe dream.

"I received a letter from Lieut. Bruce the 15th of May in answer to a letter I had written home in the company; he states that He made inquiry of Lieut. (Sergt.) Wright and found that Sergt. Wright had given [it] to Sergt. Chiles. That Chiles acknowledged that he had received but had thrown them away on account of there being encumbersome on him and threw them away without looking at or opening them. Now Capt, I think that on the day that the regiment left here, Chiles was at the hospital and I told him that I was expecting many from home and that I wanted he should tell Sergt. Wright so and have him bring my mail until I could send for it: now I cannot imagine why Sergt. Chiles shall get my letters to take care of them [unclear] away without opening or asking someone to take them, saving one or two letters was not

much weight and I know that any one would have done
as small a favor as that."

In his early correspondence, John is vitriolic and outspoken about the
war. After watching scores of soldiers fall at the Battle of Antietam, he
blasts his superiors for their poor planning that resulted in unnecessary loss
of life. He pens his insights on the leadership of the day, the importance of
foresight in war, and the devastating consequences of hasty, careless, and
narrow judgment.

> *"I know we have to suffer a great deal from incom-*
> *petency of Officers we must expect to labor under disad-*
> *vantages and sacrifices must be made to Compensate for*
> *general ship[.]*
> *And I have endeavored to conceal my feelings upon*
> *a cause I could not but regret, but each day impresses me*
> *more that in war Rashness negligence or incompetency*
> *is murder[.] I am as little disposed to allow Civilians or*
> *Press mongers to criticize Generals and abuse them un-*
> *der the guise of Patriotism as any one but I cannot help*
> *saying to you that I am hartily discouraged.*
> *I would not have you suffer that our army or any*
> *portion of it was defeated at that Battle[.] But at the time*
> *and on the portion of the field I was on, we were obliged*
> *to fall back and in doing so to make a great sacrifice of*
> *valuable life and all for want of Generals for want of in-*
> *formation and precautions[.]"*

On July 17, 1862, John was promoted to first lieutenant of Company K
at Harrison's Landing. When Lt. Col. Miller was appointed colonel of the
Seventh Minnesota Infantry, his resignation caused several upward promotions. John then became first lieutenant of Company F. Despite his disappointment with the "generalship," he was a staunch supporter of General
George McClellan and laments his removal from command in 1862 by
President Lincoln. McClellan was extremely popular among Union soldiers

because they felt he understood their concerns. In the following passage, John tells of officers who are resigning at the news of McClellan's removal. He considers doing the same.

> *Before we Reached hear we heard rumors that Ge-n[era]l McClelan was Removed from Command but we could not credit it[.] Yesterday we were paraded And he & his Staff Road along our lines to bid us farewell. I will not presume to tell you what I feel or what is the feeling of this Army and you cannot imagine it But we all feel as one man with the Strength of 100,000[.] I will not predict what the result will be But Officers by Thousands are sending their Resignations—And I hesitate betwen a dying hope of our national honor and My disgust at the knavery caprice & gulability of my fellow men which almost temps me to believe we are unfit to be free[.]*

John's support of McClellan, a Democrat who ran against Abraham Lincoln in the 1864 election, comes back to bite him later in life in the form of criticism when he returns to Winona after the war and pursues politics.

In another letter from 1862, he despondently reflects on how the Civil War will one day be viewed by historians:

> *"I think the future Historian will not fail to be impartial in his criticism on the conception and execution of this war, for it will be so difficult for him to locate the source of failure that he will attribute it to the imbecility of the whole people and call it General ignorance and congratulate their posterity that they knew no more or they might have done worse[,] for surely those who know the most are most arrogant & corrupt[.]*

A lengthy letter written from Fortress Monroe Hospital in 1862, where John was recuperating from what probably was tuberculosis, has a lighter tone and offers glimpses into John's character. He peppers his accounts with philosophical, religious, and humorous asides and pokes fun at himself.

"Again I say that I hope you will not on account of the serious tone of this letter imagine me turned monk. Metaphysics is one thing and war is another. I do not often mix them up but when I do I am in the hospital," he jests.

"This life is a school where souls are educated. One of the important branches here taught is humility and all the axioms of this study are derived from disappointment," he opines at another point.

But by 1863, a pivotal year in the war, his letters begin to assume a new and different tone.

The 1861 Letter

[1861]
Head Quarters Company "K"
1ˢᵗ Reg[imen]t Minn. Vols Camp Stone [Maryland]

Dear Parents

   *I suppose you have thought the short & hurried let-
ter which I wrote you from Alexandria some time about
the 10ᵗʰ of July was unworthy of a reply[.] If you thought
so I will say that I fully concur with you and I did not
write for the purpose of obtaining an answer but because
I thought it a duty to inform you of my whereabouts[.]*

   *Knowing I should soon see the dreaded sight and
experience the dangers of a heavy Battle I thought it a
matter of justice to inform you of so much that if I was
not permitted to address you again you could presume
upon my probably fate and also to speak of those subjects
which belonged to you to know concerning my peculiary
matters and The Last Will & Testament which I transmitted to you from Fort Snelling. I had hoped to hear*

25

from you in regard to its safe arrival & receipt by you[.] And I hope however uninteresting or short this may be you will write me—and inform me if you have received The paper of which I speak.

The reason of so short a letter at the time I wrote you last was the multitude of heavy & constant duties and the want of time[.] And such is in a great measure the case at present.

We are now encamped Two miles from Edwards Ferry on the Potomac River in General Stone's division of the upper Potomac.

Col. Gorman of the 1ˢᵗ Minnesota is in command of this Brigade. Lieut. Col. Miller is in command of The Regiment.

Capt. Lester of Company "K" is Adjutant General of the Brigade.

Our duty now is heavy Picket duty on the Potomac River or on the canal, which runs along side of the river[.] The Enemy's pickets are on the oposite side of the River, and as it (the river) is only about 351 yards wide the firing Between the Pickets is sometimes very Brisk but as yet none of the Enemy's shots have Taken Effect. We have in this Brigade stationed at Edward's Ferry 2 Regiments of infantry 1 company of Cavalry and a company of field Artillery composed of six pieces[.]

It is my impression that the Enemy are playing exactly the same game as ourselves[.] After the Defeat at the battle of Bulls run it was thought probable the Enemy would follow up their advantage by a movement into Maryland hoping if not succesful in Getting Washington at Least to cary the secession arms into the State of Maryland and redeam her from the t[h]ra[l][l]dom of The Tyrant Lincoln. Therefore the movement of our forces was at once for defense and properly so, hence, the extending of our lines by Brigades stationed along the upper Potomac.

creations in italics

The Enemy at the same time that they longed for the opertunity or power to place their arms in Maryland feared another advance of the US Army[.] They anticipated the design to move by different routes instead of one collum And that we would cross the river at different Points betwen Washington & Harpers Ferry[.] They have therefore Brought a like force to this place for The purpose of opposing us.

But we are in expectation of an attack by them and that they will plant their Batteries & attempt to cross the river[.]

And it is Safest for us to anticipate this And I only hope they will do So[.] But I do not think they are such fools as to undertake it.

I cannot spend the time to give a description of The Battle of Bulls Run with what you have doubtless obtained by reading you have formed a better Idea of it than I could in a short space [unclear] give you.

But you can be assured the fight was Bitter and The Retreat was the Superlative Degree of the same[.]

I have not been perfectly well Since and was not very well before But I am recovering very fast.

Our company is out on Picket Guard Today and to night.

I shall as Soon as I finish this Go down and Stay with them to night. I have not been out on Picket here and it is said to be interesting.

Lieut. Holzborn has Just Sent up for a Tent to be ocupied as the Head Quarters as the house at the ferry formerly used as Such is in danger of Being knocked to pieces at the first shot of the Enemy. Please Give my Kindest Regards to all.

I would I had the time to communicate to you my Ideas of the moral & Religious Bearing of this Great Struggle and The destiny of this country as a people and a nation in The event of the concession and relinquishing of our cause and results to Grow from a Victory and Overthrow of Political Cut Throats who have thus poisoned The nation to its very vitals. But time or space does not permit me to enlarge.

Again Give my love to all[.] tell the Friends I should be happy to hear from Them[.] Write me soon Direct as follows[.]

Wm P Ball
John Ball
East Rodman
Orderly Sergt
New York
Company "K"
1st Regt Minnesota Vols.
Washington DC

PS Please tell me in your reply who from Jeff County are in the army and in what regts Or what Regiments were mostly made up from That part if any.

J Ball

I Ask sister Agnes once more to Write me. Antonette is of course to much ocupied with Willie. I also wish to ask George if he never corresponds with his friends. JB

The 1862 Letters

Fortress Monroe Hospital
Wednesday Apr 16th 1862

Dear Parents

I have sumoned energy (if such an effort require that quality) to occupy a few of these weary moments in writing you and praying the debt which has been so long due[.] But where one in looking back all along the road to his present existence sees so many debts standing against his name which he can never expect to pay the mere entry of a letter due does not seam to be much acct against him[.] I confess I have sometimes felt a little murmuring of concience in regard to my correspondence with you[,] but I always silenced it by pleading inconvenience for the present and promising to repair the wrong when opportunity afforded[.]

Well I hope as a regular Irishman would that because I am writing from a hospital you will not think I am killed or mortally wounded[.]

I think the last time I wrote you I was still sojourning at Camp Stone near Edds Ferry [unclear]. [I]n fact I know it was. We left about or on the 25th of February and I suppose my diary would be about as good as any thing I could copy to make a letter compleet[.] But I will condense it and you can get some idea of the way we have been chasing that man who struck Billy Patterson[.]

Saturday March 1st
Reg[imen]t was mustered[.] I was not present acting as Provost Marshal of Harper's Ferry

Sunday March 9th 1862
Was officer of Picket Guard at Charlestown[.][M]ade the acquntance of Patrick family and several Secesch Ladies

Monday 10th
March to Berryville, had skirmish with enemy

Thursday 13th
Division marched to Winchester order countermanded marched back same day to Berryville

Friday 14th
Marched to Charlestown

Saturday 15th
Marched to Bolivar Heights in rain and sleet caught severe cold camping on spungy ground

Friday 21st
Move quarters of regiment down town on acct of sickness but had to march back immedeally on account of marching orders received for next day. Was hardly able to move

Sunday 22nd
Marched at daylight to Sandy Hook took the [unclear] for Washington arrived at Washington at midnight, a tedious day

Sunday 23rd
Officer of police guard and "sick as a dog everybody drunk and camp scattered all over town"

Monday 24th
Stayed at quarters, used up with cold

Thursday 27th
Stayed in quarters nearly all day sick [unclear]. Marched at 10 P.M for Alexandria. Arrived and suffered 3 hours on the ground 'till break of day

Thursday 28th
Marched out to old campground found it wet, felt very bad, got quarters at Mr. Martin's

Sunday 30th
Marched to Alexandria and embarked onboard the Jenny Lind amid snow and cold. Departed and anchored for the night 12 miles below

Tuesday April 1st 1862
Sailed before day light and entered the bay after the morning [unclear] it cleared up and was pleasant all day[.] Arrived at Fortress Monroe about 4 o'ck

Wednesday 2d
Sailed to Hampton and disembarked, went into Bivouac and remained sick in bed

Thursday 3d
Was too sick for duty and remained in my bed

Friday 4th
Regiment moved with [unclear] today. I was unable to march and came to hotel at Fortress Monroe

Saturday 5th
Stayed at hotel

Sunday 6th
Stayed at hotel and seemed to get worse

Monday 7th
Same

Tuesday 8th
Doct came over this morning examined my lungs and [unclear] the hospital I went

Now I have given you the outlines of my history for some time past[.] And in this you can be sure, I have felt more mortification[,] more anxiety[,] and more home and heartsickness than you can imagine.

It seames to me as if I could afford to be very sick and double the time when I get through with this campaign before if I am destined to get through. And I had rather be destined not to get through than to be cooped up here within sound of the cannon at Yorktown. Although there has been no great fight opened there yet there will soon be one of the greatest on Record.

Our Regiment has been especialy chosen and Honored by Gen[eral] McClelan and I had rather be shot than not to be with them in the hour when he calls upon them[.] The doctors tell me I can be able to go to my Regiment in 3 or 4 days and they have told me so ever since I have been here[.] I have recovered from the feaver which I had when I came here but my cough which is tireble still hangs to me[.][I]t sometimes almost strangles me and sometime before I can expectorate I cough so violent as to produce vomiting[.]

I know my cough is somewhat better but at times in my anxiety to get to my Regiment I almost fail to see it.

This they call Bronchitis which is only an inflamation of the Bronchial tubes and the mucus membrane of the lungs[.] But from some of the symptoms and the emaciated frame which has come over me in so short a time I am almost inclined to think it is genuine old white faced consumption. If this is the case I should feel like going to Yorktown in any event upon economical principles alone[.] [A] shorter road to the same place would save trouble and the doctors bill. Well a great deal is jest so you must borrow no trouble on my account[.] I shall certainly be able to join my Regiment in a few days and that is what makes me most anxious to be there before the fight for I should hate to come to them just after they had been badly cut up and achieve a dear Bought Victory. But in any event, God's will be done[.] If it is my lot to die by decease I shall try to meet it as herocaly as I can and as to the time and manner it is a secondary consideration[.] The fact is cirtain that at some time in some maner the Lord that gave will take away and who shall say he is not wise blessed be the name of Lord. Well most of my letter thus far has been concerning myself[.] Now I must speak of others. I owe a Thousand Appologies to Antoinette[.] I shall not censure her a particle if she should discard me as an inconstant brother and undeserving of further attention[.]

She has, I confess, much reason to think if I was an uncharitable and ungrateful Boy. I am unnaturaly indiferant to a sisters kindness as a man[.] Please give her my love and also George (if he is a man who loves his whole country to well to have it torn assunder). Kiss Willie and tell him about his _mithical_ uncle John. I say _mithical_ because he never has [unclear] may see me.

I do not know what to say to or of Agnes. I cannot tell how to adress her. I look at her as I have looked at the pelican on the placid lakes of Minnesota. The reflections of their white bodies upon the smooth water with so large and pearly white in the slight angle of incidence and reflection that I could not tell how much of the bird was above the water and how much beneath or which was bird and which was shadow. So I view the growing mind and opening faculties of that sister Agnes on the smooth waters where I at present see her. My allowance for her growth and progress which the change of years must have brought no reflection or image to my mind of the proportions of her soul or intellect. Well I cannot really tell you how much is in the image and how much of the bird is above the water. So although I believe I ought to know my sister, I cannot feel that I know Agnes.

I suppose I can imagine pretty well how things are moving generally. Uncle H. continues business in town. Grandpapa is with them. Uncle Talott is as usual, living very comfortable but a little dissatisfied with his present situation.

Uncle Calvin, as usual, enforming the good will and confidence of all who know him, and the favor of God. Of course not free from the ribald caprise of the ill bred. I think you told me in your last that Ruth Yondes had experienced the religion of Jesus Christ. I am rejoiced to hear or if and she shall ever have my prayers for a continuance of his grace and the [unclear] of his spirit which shall make her feel in all of the sisitudes of this world that she can fasten her hopes there and they will not fail. I have ever felt since I saw Ruth a young woman, and so different from other members of the family a deep sympathy for her in her evident mortification and sorrow, and had it been in my power, as I had reason to suppose *it would be, I should certainly have served her to prepare herself for a high position in intellectual and social attainments and enabled her to command what her marriage deserved. This plan kindly meant like a thousand other dreaming realities was lost like a [unclear] in a dream. When a little wind blows the breath of fate, it bursts the bubble.*

Well I presume you think I write strangely, and think my mind runs to contemplation of melancholy subject and I court a somber mood. But if so, you are mistaken. Some subjects lead one to those veins of plot. No I am more cheerful, lighthearted, and gay than ever. But I have learned some things that many do not learn, that there is no certainty in human plans. But human plans are all proper and necessary, but a man must not have his affections on them. If this be permitted, it frustates the aim and ends which God designed for man and all men sooner or later must find out this one truth, and happy is the man who first by experience becomes satisfied and rests upon this milestone and reads "seek yee first the kingdom of God and Christ." Do you say I am a man who have met with dissapointment? That my temper is soured and my reasoning perverted? Not so. This life is a school where souls are educated. One of the important branches here taught is humility and all the axioms of this study are derived from dissapointment.

I call this religious knowledge. Derived from the experience which enables us to look through nature up to nature's God. This knowledge of the uncertainty event does not discourage or dishearten or fill the mind with gloomy anticipation of the furture in life, but encourages in all the lottable pursuits of life, and if they succeed for a while—alls well and if they fail, a placid resignation to the will of God is a happy termination. I feel prepared to spend life now like as a man. I could better serve my fellow man and my God than ever before. I hope that in the

*future I meet my dissapointments which could afflict me
as in some of my earlier lessons and where ardent hope
and expectation are not placed about subjects and interest which all men feel uncertain. The mind suffers not the
doubt and tremor of the mind which is ever conscious of
doubt and uncertainty of the objects of its affections. But
a placid security ever prevails in the soul of him whose
affections are placed on things above. Again I say that
I hope you will not on account of the serious tone of this
letter imagine me turned monk. Metaphysics is one thing
and war is another. I do not often mix them up but when
I do I am in the hospital.*

    *By the way I will relate a little occurrence which
happened to me the other morning. I was complimented
and annoyed by the appearence in my room of a recent
aquaintance. A captain of the third calvary. By the way
he proffessed one might have thought he was a physician.
He was one of those versatile scholastic men who tell
much more than they communicate. Well, he thought, I
had better get out on the [unclear] of the hospital and get
the morning air at the same time explaining that eleva-
tion gave a kind of purchase to the action of the atmo-
sphere. Malaria and [unclear], by its violent action upon
the lungs, a kind of snap opens to the vesicles of the below
thoratis. So I got the required purchase when out came
the Merrimack and a lot of little fish besides. I watched
from this conspicuous position, the movements of the
fleets, the foreign vessels and also, with a little mortification I saw one of the gunboats steal the vessels out of the
roads almost under my nose. I should not have felt a bit
more agreived if a nigger had carried off my soup of the
first course of a dinner or I had been without breakfast.*

    *Well there was no fight but I suppose you would like
to have me say what the Merrimack looks like. As far as I
could judge, she was not surpassingly beautiful. Without
going into classics or calling on my friend, the Surico*

Captain I thought of myself that she looked about like the top of a barn. I did not consult the captain for he was fluently astonishing some newcommers with the narration of his persistant refusal to go on General Mclelan's staff. He would've told the story to several officers on whom I saw him fix his eyes. But on looking at his watch he simply informed them that he must go below and dress for dinner for he promised to dine with General Wool. Well I think I scarcely have written enough to please or pester you and enough to fill and envelope so you may expect me to close soon as I have been writing all evening. I shall expect to hear from you at your earliest convenience. You must excuse penmanship, I write in all styles and degrees except the comparitave and the superlative. Please give my regards to all and love to all who can expect the expression and permit me to remain as ever, your affectionate son, John Ball.

Mr. and Mrs. W.P. Ball

Direct Lieutenant John Ball First Minnesota Regiment Army of the Potomac

I was near the 35th New York and was too unwell to go and see them. I made the aquaintance of Captain Schaffer of the 34th Regiment. I expect to see them so when I shall probably meet Allan Adson. Again, goodbye, John Ball

✳ ✳ ✳

Camp Bolivar Heights Va
Sept 25th 1862

Dear Parents

Some time has elapsed since I have written or heard from you and it would take a great while to tell you all the varying circumstances and heavy labors it has been my fortune to experience since our last correspondence[.] I tell you there is not as much history in your whole life time as in a week of such campaigning[.] I will not attempt to tell you any thing[.] I know It would be inseperable in its interest to You and it would require to long a letter to tell you all[.] As for danger I will only say I have been as Rear guard on the Peninsula Retreat, went out to Centreville to save [General] Pope. Was rearguard of one column from Vienna to Fairfax via Vienna to Chain Bridge moved out from Washington to give the Invaders a touch in Maryland had a light skirmish with them near Frederick and fought them at the Battle of Antietam and at last after we have partly scared and partialy fought the enemy out of Maryland we are permitted to go into Bivouac and for two days I have had the first Rest I have experienced since I left Harrisons Landing during that time I have been engaged in 2 Armed recognizances 2 Skirmishes 2 Brilliant little fights and repulsed the attacks of the enemy on our rear and in One Battle But these are but little of the Heavy labor and long fatiguing marches the movements on transports the continued anxiety and exposure which cannot be told[.] Company "K" with whom I was on duty until we Reached Frederick lost 4 Killed besides Capt Holzborn who was Killed at Antietam[,] 2 wounded and 3 Taken prisoner.

In the last Battle they lost 3 fine fellows Killed besides the Captain and 7 wounded 4 seriously Since Frederick and in the Battle I was in command of Co. "F" as I am now a first Lieut and in command of that Company. I lost 3 killed, 4 wounded, and one missing. My second Lieut. is sick and was at that time[.] I have some satisfaction *in Knowing that though we were obliged to retire and under a destructive fire of infantry and artillery it was no fault of ours and the men under my command as also all our regt showed a willingness to stay till the last man was shot down[.]*

But I am hartily discouraged when I review the generalship not of the command[er] in chief or his staff[.] I of course could see but part but I find no fault with that with division & corps commanders[.]

I saw Gen[.] Patrick formerly Major Patrick[,] Just as I was going on to the field. But have not had the opportunity to see or hear of him since[.]

He had a collumn lying down in the woods and skirmishers in front where we took our position and received our first fire[.]

I soon discovered our line breaking or the regt on our left falling back in disorder and the Enemy's fire soon followed them over the Ridge and came in directly on our left and we were ordered to fall back and the flank fire of the Enemy drove the Broken ranks back in a mass upon Patrick's reserves in such a manner that I think he could not use them and I am doubtful if his reserves were in a position to be made available to support the line where it gave way[.]

But the Error was in the Division and corps Commander[.] They did not know what they had to do and made no disposition and prepared for no emergencies[.]

I know we have to suffer a great deal from incompetency of Officers we must expect to labor under disadvantages and sacrifices must be made to Compensate for general ship[.]

And I have endeavored to conceal my feelings upon a cause I could not but regret, but each day impresses me more that in war Rashness negligence or incompetency is murder[.] I am as little disposed to allow Civilians or Press mongers to criticize Generals and abuse them under the guise of Patriotism as any one but I cannot help saying to you that I am hartily discouraged.

I would not have you suffer that our army or any portion of it was defeated at that Battle[.] But at the time and on the portion of the field I was on, we were obliged to fall back and in doing so to make a great sacrifice of valuable life and all for want of Generals for want of information and precautions[.] I only have to renew my thanks that I am again permitted to continue the correspondence which has ceased while these movements have been progressing[.] In comparative health & free from harm. I remain as Ever yours,

Wm P. Ball John Ball

You must excuse Bad penmanship[.] I have written this lying on my side in my tent and my paper Resting on my blankets[.] Such a position is a luxury JB

❄ ❄ ❄

Camp Warrenton Va—
Nov. 11ᵗʰ 1862

Dear Parents

I wrote you from Harpers Ferry on the Evening of the 29ᵗʰ [unclear] and promised to write you again from the field[.] I now take this opportunity to review the proceedings of the past 12 days and to assure you of my health and disposition[.] You will of course excuse my writing you with a pencil sitting on the ground floor of my tent and holding my paper on my knee[.]

On the 30ᵗʰ as anticipated or partially anticipated we marched crossed the Shenandoah and at about 6 miles camped in a grove near Schnickers Gap[.] General

Plesenton was in our front and Kept up a brisk and continuous fire upon the Enemy who were retiring before us[.]

We Remained through the 31st & made Muster Rolls and passed inspection & muster[.] On the 1st inst we marched down to schnickers gap and took position somewhat expecting Battle[.] On the 2d we found to use an old darkeys expression that the Enemy had Advanced 7 miles back And we occupied the Gap[.] This was sunday and at night we Advanced 3 miles on the East side of the mountains leaving one Division to hold the Gap we moved forward toward where Pleasanton was skirmishing with the Rear of the Enemy his guns continued their roar till late at night[.] On the 3d the cannonading was resumed on both sides we moved forward and found the Enemy's cavalry viletts at 3 oclock PM but were ordered not to bring on an engagement so we only slightly pressed their left and forced them to fall back Rapidly Through Ashbys Gap Gen[eral] Pleasanton giving them some severe work at dark[.] On the 4th we made Recognizance through the gap and found it abandoned by enemy. Gen[eral] McClelan came up with his staff to the crest of the mountain and remained 2 hours watching the enemys field operations & line of Retreat as from this point we have a fine view of the Shenandoah Valley[.] 5th we remained at the little town of Paris at the Entrance of Ashbys Gap guarding it while our army moved on down on the East of the mountains.

On the sixth we moved as Rearguard to a very long train[.] Gen[era]l Sullys Brigade and one Battery about 4 miles and took position and remained to guard a cros Road.

On 7th Remained in same position[.] Quite cold and today we experienced our first snow[.]

On the 8th we moved forward about 2 ½ miles to the Camp of the Trains one Army Corps[.] Hear we remained all day a cold, bleak day waiting for the trains to get out of our way the train was so extensive that it was after dark when the last wagon started and we marched and all the early part of the night the rear of this immense train was delayed by bad Roads and we marched a few Rods and halted and about 11 ock we came to better Roads and had a good march about 2 miles When The Battery upset one of their caissons and Broke the Trail[.] This caused a delay of about 2 hours and the train on good Roads got out of our way And we marched Straight through within about 6 miles of Waranton some 10 miles and arrived about 3 ock in the morning[.]

At Sunrise we were called out to march to this place in Advance of the train and Arrived at about 10 ock[.] Yesterday the 10th was the most memorable day we have experienced during the war[.] Before we Reached hear we heard rumors that Gen[era]l McClelan was Removed from Command but we could not credit it[.] Yesterday we were paraded And he & his Staff Road along our lines to bid us farewell. I will not presume to tell you what I feel or what is the feeling of this Army and you cannot imagine it But we all feel as one man with the Strength of 100,000[.] I will not predict what the result will be But Officers by Thousands are sending their Resignations— And I hesitate betwen a dying hope of our national honor and My disgust at the knavery caprice & gulability of my fellow men which almost temps me to believe we are unfit to be free[.]

I do not know what I shall do [unclear] when in the face of [unclear] and the report of cannon has been heard All day and I am told The Enemy are advancing upon us[.] I know If I should resign I shall be subjected to a Reproach for resigning in the face of the Enemy[.] And yet I feel that we are fighting against Time and against hope. I cannot conceive the meaning of the last act[.]

But you need not be surprised to hear of me either in Richmond or Rutland[.] remain as Ever yours

Father & Mother John Ball

✳ ✳ ✳

Camp near Falmouth Va
Dec 5th 1862

Dear Parents

Whenever convenient since I left you to mark out the devious track of social independence I have on my birth day wrote you a letter[.] At first these letters if not hopeful in expression were well disguised for I will remember the feelings and sentiments which inspired all my acts of that period[.] I have for some time been accustomed to occupy this day in summing up and comparing the progress of my life if not its improvements[.] I have sometimes felt so well satisfied that I am now surprised [unclear] feelings I then experienced perhapse caused by the vigor of my imagination[.] At other times I was peculiarly depressed and considered my fate an extremely hard one [.] Today has not been peculiarly different from most of the days I experience in the occupation[.]

We are now in camp about ¾ of a mile above Falmouth which you know is on the Rappahannock river opposite Fredericksburg[.] We have been here now some three weeks, our camp is quite comfortable considering that we lack many things which the [unclear] department should supply us with, many things seam to indicate that we would stay here some time[.] Hookers and Franklins ground divisions have moved and as this is the line of supplies it would seam as if this was to be made a kind of line

43

of defense and this point an eventual base to the army in advance and it is at least all important crossing and must be well guarded by a large detachment to secure the safty of an advance movement which I think will undoubtedly soon be made if not already commenced[.] I know if we stay here a while the probability of our being engaged in a great battle soon is much lessened. But with such a force and so ably [unclear] as that in our front we may at any moment in our movement [unclear] them to take the offense and we shall then likely have the heavyest part of the campaign[.]

However I am perfectly willing to stop at this point[.] I shall not feel the least slight if left behind[.] I can only repeat when I review the past and survey the future I am disquieted and my disgust is so complete that I am ½ demoralized[.] If I was compelled to look upon our cause as hopeless[,] I might still have some consolation that it was no falt of ours[.] But as it is if our cause is not hopeless it is no falt of ours[.] And if we are in the end successful[,] I shall not experience the satisfaction from it that I would if we had achieved our success[.] When I review the conduct of this war[,] I cannot find a branch an exception to the defective systems which pervades the whole and when I say war system I mean the whole governance system[,] for all its branches are now directed to the war[,] and since I am on this subject and I may be permitted to express my mind on that which is nearest my heart once in the year[,] at least I will venture to speak planely and dispassionately[.]

I think the future Historian will not fail to be impartial in his criticism on the conception and execution of this war, for it will be so difficult for him to locate the source of failure that he will attribute it to the imbecility of the whole people and call it General ignorance and congratulate their posterity that they knew no more or they might have done worse[,] for surely those who know the most are most arrogant & corrupt[.]

I will probably hurt the feelings of some by calling the free educated and litterary mass of American people Ignorant[.] Shall I explain a learned man may yet be an ignorant man and may be more dangerous than a fool for he lacks the key stone of all all knowlage.

Knowlage is for use and and the learned is ignorant unless they know, How to use it[.]

I received a letter from E[.] Thompson they day before yesterday[.] [H]e was somewhat pleased with the removal of General McClelan[.] Says he can[']t go into the street without being insulted[.] Is accused of squandering the Best Blood of the country and all the money he wanted he feels indignant and won[']t let McClelan stay in Command of the army "What cause." [H]e is a democrat and is not as successful as we hoped[.] We[']ll turn him out and put another democrat in who has not done as much according to his Blood and Money as Genl McClelan[.] I suppose he means by this cause for McClelans Removal that Burnside will soon bee superseded by some one else. Well when the indignant people at home have superseded until they get some Break neck cuss some true Representative of themselves to throw aside all principles old acknowlaged principles and one who will just pitch in like Pope disreguarding all lines of defence, Depots of Supplies, Base of Opperations, & be brought to a close[.] I am almost certain it will then. I hope the indignant people will feel than this revenge is satisfactory[.]

I would not speak this in disrespect or contempt of Edd's views[.] I know they are common among inteligent and devout lovers of our country[.] I only say what I do if possible to convince you and all that no army can ever be successful when commanded by a popular will or according to the dictates of a council of war consisting of multitudes of diverse interests[,] partisan prejudices[,]

45

different schools of philosophy[,] and capricious ignorance with sensation newspapers for their reports on Mitchels or McNalleys [unclear] for their statistics[.] I tell you if there is not patriotism enough in this country and faith enough in the Rulers (I mean the new of authority) to furnish money and men[,] and I rush to them and the men who success or sympathy gives to direct them[,] the country is not worth saving or the people fit to be free[.]

I say success and long and Honorable Service and un-explainable and instructive sympathy between soldiers and their Generals will point out the men who should lead them[.]

And a people not insane and in sympathy with the army will never rejoice when their favorite general is taken from them in the Hour of Reverses and in the face of `the enemy when boom of the cannon is sounding all day around the moving columns of a large army show-ing how near the enemy is in force contesting the ground with the advances[.] Any one who is no [unclear] and has any conception of the moral on the Esprit de Corps of an army under a tried and favorite General can see this[.] Whatever the people may feel privately they should know that an army is subject to demoralization in the hour of Reverse[,] and if they lose confidence in their General[,] they are almost worthless[.] But if they retain their attach-ment and confidence[,] the people may feel confidence in them. Never in such an hour take that confidence from them[.]

The proper provnice of the people at home represent their opinions through the civil authorities to the army as to the character of the war the objects to be attained give moral tone and [unclear] noble deeds and good dis-eplin[,] but let them never directly or indirectly strive to interfear with the acts of plans of a General Courts of Inquiry or Court Martial are a ready means to criticize & punish, and these will be used enough in a country where

46

military rivalry and desire for promotion is based more upon the feelings of others than merits in themselves[.]

I feel it is a great presumption in me to criticize the acts of an independent commander in the field[,] and still more when I know how he is directed by the [unclear] council[,] though I feel myself as well qualified to do so as any of my old acquaintances[.] I have seen some things which looked surprising to me on the part of Generals now high in command[.] But I could not and cannot now think but that they were the cause of failures[.] But perhaps I did not see all the combinations[.] I cannot tell[,] but that which I considered an almost unpardonable blunder was no neglect or want of Generalship[,] and I may have been intentional and the fault somewhere else no notice was taken of it afterwards though well and externaly known. I am sure the people at home who only hear what the papers & [unclear] say and are themselves incapacitated have no grounds to pass judgment[.] I would not propose a plan of campaign to a general if I could[.][I]f he could execute his own[,] he could not mine because he would be my aid at camp and could not fully conceive my plan[,] however good[.] I will not criticize the Generals[,] for they are recommended to be above criticism or below a court martial[,] but I will criticize this popular egotism[,] this manufacture of Generals[,] this lavish of high rank upon political unskillful corrupt & cowardly aspirants for honorable distinction[.] I will criticize the property of national military committees who assume to pass upon the capacities of fitness of civilians for officers and the acts of an officer of the army in a military capacity when a military man cannot hold the office from which they assume the power to judge him[.] And in civilized countries a man may claim the right to be judged by his peers[.]

Misfortunes in war are to be anticipated[.] History does not contain the account of a single General of note however sublime the close of his career [unclear] may secure the course of his victories & conquests[.] But what the Military Commentation or scholar points out his temporary disasters and some place where a mistake in the acts of his enemy saved him from inglorious defeat or an overthrow of his plans[.] Many of the disasters to the greatest military leaders of history must have been more disheartening to the people at home and gave greater cause of complaint to the country than any of the most unfortunate affairs of this war[.] Would you have your Frederick your Eugene your Charles or your Napoleon deprived of command on such grounds[?]

Can any good come from a system of Aulic Councels Military Commissions instituted to quiet the clamor of the people and compelled by public opinion to report according to the direction given by a few isolated facts end the testimony of those who wish to shift the blame to other shoulders[?] Can any good come from a committee who report that the forces were sufficient at Harpers Ferry and no excuse can serve the commanders at that point[?] A stigma is left upon the name of the dead commander and the Ranking officer under him is dismissed the service and in the same report censores the commander of an army for not reinforcing it[.]

And while the people of the country are censoring Genl McClelan for not making his victory more complete [unclear] where all was engaged. They read with approval the report which says he should have drawn from that force to reinforce a position already strong enough[.]

All that was wanted of the commanders at Harpers Ferry was to hold that position[,] and if Col Miles & Ford where censurable[,] Gen McClenan was not[.]

I know no military system but this where everybody or nobody is blameable of a single fault[.] One year ago a senatorial committee was called to satisfy the insulted people by an investigation of the Battles of Balls Bluff[.]

[N]othing was discovered to found even censure upon against Genl Stone[,] and it was considered an unfortunate affair[.] But the people became fearfuly excited after the thing was over[.][W]e thought we saw some fault at the time[,] but could not realy blame General Stone[.] [B]ut some things looked strange[.] Genl Stone was a [unclear] soldier[,] he never went before his orders [unclear] the public mind for them or followed after to explain or appoligize for them[.] Soon he was Relieved of Command and sent to Fort Leafayette[.] The army Regulations & articles give him as speedy trial upon charges performed within 10 days from his arrest[.] But he was some 8 months in prison and then Released and never knew and does not now know upon what grounds he was arrested[.][H]e beget a court of inquiry and demanded trials in vain[.][H]e said if they will not give me back my command[,] let me go to the Peninsular and fight in the ranks as a private[.] How often have this division spoke without a discordant voice[,] "I wish they would give us Genl Stone again[.] I am willing to put myself in his hands at a juncture[.]" I might follow this style of citing [unclear] to show how completely ineffectual are our labors and demonstrate which disgusts and [unclear] the army[.] Do not think I overrate it[.] I do not so much blame the people[.] They believe the lies the papers tell[.]

Each issue it assumes the people that soon they will have to record the downfall of Richmond & the [unclear] of the President[,]" there now you have let them get away again[.]" "Why don't you take this thing into your own hands[.]" If a mistake is made arrest and [unclear] the officer "If a plan fails discipline Our Brave soldiers shall no longer suffer and [unclear] on account of failures[.]"

On the day I write the Herald publishes the correspondence from Washington & the army saying the preparations are nearly completed you may expect soon the

Battle of the war and Rebelion its death blow[.] Richmond will be ours befr the 1ˢᵗ of January[.]

There has no dissatisfaction in the army of the Potamac on account of McClelans Removal[.]

War Department Reports that no Regulations have been tendered on account of the Removal of Genl McClelan [end of letter—final pages missing]

✳ ✳ ✳

U.S. Hospital, Patent Office.
Washington, D.C. Dec. 12ᵗʰ 1862

Sir,

Please forward to me by return mail the <u>Descriptive List</u>, with <u>pay and clothing account</u> of Private Edwin Season of your Company, who is now in the Hospital.

The clothing account must give the money value of the clothing, drawn from State and Federal Government.

Very respectfully,
To Commander
Jas D. Robison
of Com. F. 1ˢᵗ Regt.
Surgeon U.S. Vols.
Minnesota Vols.
In charge of Hospitals

✳ ✳ ✳

Camp near Falmouth Va—
Dec 25ᵗʰ Christmas 1862

Dear Mother & Sister

Yours of the 9th and 14th came to hand on the 23rd and was received while on picket[.] I wrote on the 17th to tell you I was safe & well but did not say much on the subject of matters here and you need not be surprised if I do not say much surprised if I say nothing bout it now for it would be better satisfaction to me and probably would only add to your solicitude and anxiety without holding out to you the prospect of any thing better in the future—

I have not received any letter since Antoinette was married which was so satisfactory in the news it contained as in yours & the last I received from E. Thompson[.]

I suppose if I should tell you some things which are secrets to you to day it will be no secret when you receive this But I will tell you. Last Evening Alfred Isham was married. Tonight My old friend Harlan Dunlap is to be married to Miss Martha Hopkins[.] Now if by any failure in the arrangements the news papers do not record this movements or no such action takes place you may consider there is some failure in the plans and in such case you need not say any thing about it.

I was somewhat surprised to find that Marcellus Monroe was to be married at this time and I had to think some time before I could recolect who Janette Blackstone was, but I remember she was the Widow of Seeander Smith. Were it not for the statement calling to mind her history. I had forgoten that he was dead[.] I was somewhat surprised and could hardly realize the general tone of Agness letter[.] I could hardly believe that Charley Eames was teaching school[.] Although I know he is old enough if he has made good progress to warrant him competent but I saw him but 4 years ago and it seams as if he was yet but a mear boy[.]

What is Henry Eames doing—

I thought when I left home the last time that unless duty called me I should never want to visit it again[.] But now I feel differently I know I could enjoy myself if I could visit you and my friends as well as those who ought to have been my friends and from <u>my</u> <u>own faults</u> were not my friends[.]

I am now prepared to witness changes for I know all things change and I would not prevent it[.]

I do wish to see the good and Kind old people who have ever manifested an interest in my welfare as well as the young who are making progress to fill their places and now in the same relation and situation in regard to the old that I once occupied[.]

I call to mind many who will ever claim me their debtor and I know from their Kindness and Nobility of nature all who have the benefit of their society will have the same obligations to pay[.]

I have not had the opportunity to know what is the fate of Allen Adsit since recent action and I have so much on hand now for a few days I shall not be able to visit him as he is in another Corps and grand division[.]

I do not know when I shall come home if ever from present appearances. I think [it] doubtful if I can ever get leave of absence and if at all not for a sufficient length of time to visit home[.] Scarce any leave of absence is granted by Old Sumner.

Many Officers have never left the Regiment a day and no reasons can procure an approval of <u>Old Disapproval</u>[.]

I understand David Eames & Moris Read are in an artillery Regiment and I rather suppose they are with Banks[.] Let me know if you know where they are. If it is light Artillery tell me what Battery and where assigned[.]

Give my love to Mr. Eameses people and All the Relatives & friends[.]

Write Soon

John Ball

Miss Agnes & Mrs. DA Ball
1ˢᵗ Leiut Comg. Co. "F"
East Rodman New York
1ˢᵗ Minnesota Vols

Now Agnes, You see we can exchange letters once each month and I shall expect to keep up the correspondence, unless circumstances prevent. JB

Courtesy of Wayne Jorgenson

Sacrifices at Gettysburg and Bristoe Station

By the spring of 1863, the sometimes caustic, damning tone in John's letters has softened. His long marches, bloody battles, and burying of the dead seem to have resulted in an air of detached acceptance. The battlefield increasingly has become an opportunity for analytical observation.

"Thus I waited like a spectator at a public execution for I knew they would attack Sedgwick and overpower him by a superior force from all sides," he writes after predicting the outcome of the Battle of Salem Church, which he observes from a distance. The Union forces incurred sizable losses there due to the poor judgment of Maj. Gen. Joseph Hooker, who he clearly loathed, calling him untrustworthy, egotistical, and a braggart. After reading Hooker's congressional testimony, John fumes about the general:

> *"I never read anything so unjust, unreasonable, false, and egotistical as that testimony. And I tell you such a man is not to be trusted even if he had the ability. And he that is so wise in his own concept and sits in judgment with so little scruples and hesitation upon them must certainly never have thought of the doubtful questions that arise to a candid mind. I tell you if he wins, which he may do, it will be because his army wins in spite of him."*

By comparison he speaks of the First Minnesota's Col. William Colvill, who led the initial charge against the oncoming Confederates at Gettysburg, with humorous affection. Colonel Colvill was greatly admired by his troops.

> "In personal he is a monster. You can judge of his height in comparison with mine.... The representation in the picture is nothing compared to what he is when he straightens himself (which he sometimes does height.) 6'4" in his stockings. A capacity for aleing and drinking that has not been known since the days of Maximilian. A faithful follower of Rip Van Winkle and David Crockett."

In the 1863 letters, there are details of marching orders, picket duty, and the grind of daily life. One senses conditions are unbearable at times as the troops pass through the autumn equinox storms without tents or blankets, and endure long, dusty marches.

"I am in excellent health or I could not have stood this march," he writes in a June 17, 1863, letter on the road to Gettysburg. "I have seen many fall in spasm from heat and exertion and I suppose we have lost hundreds who were not able to come through. And the ambulances were not sufficient.... You have doubtful heard that the enemy is in Pennsylvania." John had been marching with the 2nd Army Corps for nearly a month. Capt. John McCallum had been wounded in the foot in Dec. 1862 at the Battle of Fredericksburg. This effectively put First Lieutenant John Ball in command of Company F. By May 1863, McCallum was transferred to the Veterans Reserve Corps. After the Battle of Gettysburg, on July 6th, John was promoted to the rank of captain.

On the morning of July 2, his regiment moved toward Gettysburg. By afternoon, they were on the crest of Cemetery Ridge partway down the slope. Around 4 o'clock, they began to receive harassing fire from sharpshooters on the left. Colonel Colvill ordered Company F to deploy and address the problem.

"We were only a single, little regiment—at most but 290 officers and men—posted alone on a hillside and apparently forgotten in the surge of greater events around us," wrote Sergeant Wright of Company F in his memoir "No More Gallant a Deed."

"It was already apparent that our forces were yielding and that at some points the enemy had broken through and was advancing. ... Company F (Capt. Ball) was detached and ordered to skirmish in that direction" toward Round Top, where his men fired into the Confederates as members of the Barksdale and Wilcox Brigades passed by them. With those skirmishing orders from Col. Covill, John's company averted the devastation taking place about 400 yards to their right.

"Colonel, do you see those colors?" commanding officer Major General Winfield Scott Hancock shouted out to Colvill. "Then take them!" With those orders, the First Minnesota was told to charge a Confederate regiment four times its size.

"Col. Colvill gave the orders, and the men promptly obeyed it and started on one of the most desperate and bloody, forlorn movements that any organized body of soldiers was ever ordered to attempt," Wright recalled of the First Minnesota's suicidal mission. The charge served to delay the Confederates and gain a few minutes time before Union reinforcements could relieve them.

Of the estimated 262 men that went into the charge, 215 lay killed or wounded on the field. After the fight, which lasted perhaps 15 to 20 minutes, initially only 47 men made it back to the top of the hill from which they had started, though other walking wounded gradually made their way back as well.

In the execution of this order, the First Minnesota "suffered a hitherto unheard of loss in open field fighting," Wright recalled. "It was a fearful record and it stands today without a parallel in the history of open warfare since the invention of gunpowder."

During a reunion speech at Gettysburg 30 years later, Lieutenant William Lochren of the First Minnesota recalled the call to charge the Confederates this way: "Every man realized in an instant what that order meant. Death or wounds to us all—the sacrifice of the regiment to gain a few minutes time and save the position and probably the battlefield. And every man saw and accepted the necessity for that sacrifice. Responding to Colvill's rapid orders, the regiment in perfect line, with arms at right shoulder shift, was in a moment down that slope directly in the enemy's center."

"There is no more gallant deed recorded in history," Major General Hancock later wrote. "I would have ordered that regiment in if I had known every man would have been killed. It had to be done."

Sacrificing the regiment allowed the Union Army to organize and gain critical ground. The 39th and 11th New York regiments attacked on the left of the First; the 19th Mass. and 42nd New York on the right. The First Minnesota was the only regiment that completed the charge.

Over 620,000 Americans died in the Civil War: The costliest battle was at Gettysburg, with at least 45,000 casualties. Some 23 Union regiments lost more than half their forces there. But the First Minnesota incurred the greatest casualties.

When it came time for roll call on July 2, every man in John Ball's Company F was present or accounted for. But there was intense anxiety about fellow regiment members stationed to their right: The trees had obscured their view, and they had no idea what the outcome was of the charge. Captain Ball requested permission to leave the line to search for his comrades. Permission was denied that afternoon but granted for the following morning.

Ball then sent Sergeant Hamline as a scout to check on the regiment, who reported back that only a handful of men were still alive. Company F was in disbelief: "Someone said: 'These things are always reported worse than they are—at the first. They have been separated by the fighting and are scattered in the darkness; they will turn up all right in the morning—the most of them,'" Sergeant Wright recalled.

After a few hours of sleep, Wright awoke to find Captain Ball pacing: "he said that he had been there for some time, as he had been unable to sleep for thinking. Said he had heard twice from the regiment during the night, and the loss was very great—he could not tell how great—and he was waiting permission to go to it."

Finally, permission was granted to return to their regiment. They walked down the line of soldiers "to find Capt. Nathan Messick with the colors and what was left of the regiment, 47 men who had not been hit and a few that had. We had not been separated far or long, but the greetings were as sincere and earnest as if oceans had divided us and years had elapsed. There was a flood of inquiries about the missing ones. The answers left no doubts in our minds of the awful calamity that had befallen the regiment," Wright penned.

July 3 turned out to be a particularly long day for Company F: Around 1 o'clock they began receiving "an artillery prelude to Pickett's Charge" in which every minute they expected "to be blown to atoms," Wright recorded.

> "There was an incessant, discordant flight of shells—
> seemingly in and from all directions—howling, shrieking,
> striking, exploding, tearing, smashing, and destroying—
> producing a scene that words cannot present and was well
> nigh unbearable. The ground was torn up; fences and trees
> knocked to splinters; rocks and small stones were flying
> in the air; ammunition boxes and caissons were exploded
> with a frequency we had never known before; guns were
> dismounted; and men and horses were torn in pieces, as the
> enemy's massed artillery pounded and ploughed the crest of
> the ridge where our batteries were. This ordeal lasted, we
> are told, about two hours, but it seemed to me that it was
> running on into years."

Despite the intensity of their experience, Company F came out remarkably sound, having incurred very few losses with only 2 dead and 7 wounded. After the July 3 battle, they prepared their dead comrades for burial and helped the wounded.

John led his company valiantly and wisely. "He was noted for ability, coolness and bravery," stated his Sept. 29, 1875, obituary, which ran in the "Jefferson County Journal."

The regiment was so decimated after the battle that John was shifted from Company F to captain of Company B. Several months later, he proved his bravery once again at the Battle of Bristoe Station, according to his longtime friend Martin Maginnis, who noted in an affidavit that they "messed and lived together and were in constant companionship until June 1865." Maginnis was by John's side when he was almost fatally wounded:

"The enemy advanced in several charges upon the line and once seemed about to take the railroad—when among a few others, Capt. Ball sprang in front of the line upon the embankment and firing all the shots from his revolver into the advancing enemy, threw his revolver in their faces. That just as they broke and retreated before our fire, he was shot down, by my side, as we supposed wounded—the ball passing through his groin and carrying away one of his testes. He came very close to death, but unexpectedly recovered and rejoined his regiment, though he never recovered his former vigor and superb health."

John returned to Rutland, New York, to recover from three wounds he incurred while driving about 40 prisoners through a culvert at Bristoe Station (also spelled Bristow), according to his obituary. He was one of the few Union soldiers killed or wounded there, where 322 Confederate soldiers became prisoner. "The fight was a short one, but fatal to the foe," the Winona Daily Republican reported on Oct. 22, 1863.

The 1863 Letters

U.S. Gen'l Hospital, Patent Office
Washington, D.C.
March 21, 1863

Sir:
I have to inform you that Archibald Bamber Private Company "F" 1ˢᵗ Regiment Minn. Volunteers has been paid [unclear] for the months of Jan. and Feb. 1863 at this hospital $26.

Very respectfully,
[unclear] Goober
Apt Surgeon the Vols., in charge of Hospital.
To the commander of Co "F" 1ˢᵗ Minn. Vols.

❋ ❋ ❋

Camp Falmouth Station
May 8,th 1863

Dear Parents,
    The fighting has ceased and the army as you have doubtless heard is again on the north side of the Rappahannock*[.] I am writing a few words to let you know I am all right[.] We were not seriously engaged as our division was left on this side in their old camps to do picket duty and keep up appearances while the remainder of our corps moved up to the right with the Army[.] We moved in the night and at day light laid a pontoon bridge and camped and took possession of Fredericksburg and at 10 o'clock cooperated with the 6th corps (Sedgwick's*) in carrying the heights with slight loss to us and considerable to the enemy[.]The same heights which the battle of the 13th of Dec, 1862 failed to accomplish[.] But they were not strongly defended this time we pursued the enemy a couple of miles and then our division was ordered back to this side of the river while the 6th corps followed the enemy up the plank road towards Gordonville which Gen. Hooker held seven miles in the rear[.] You may be surprised when I tell you that this success and pursuit did not afford me the least satisfaction[.] I had lost all confidence in the commanding general previous to this and I saw his plan was too apparent and could not succeed although our force as I believe was ½ greater than the enemy[.] While we were engaged, successfully heavy fighting was going on at the right, and I was satisfied it boded no good to us[.] And when we were ordered to this side of the river and Sedgwick followed and engaged the enemy heavily at 5 o'clock, I was satisfied it was to retrieve Hooker[.] Sedgwick was repulsed with considerable loss but held his position. Then I knew that the enemy having got Hooker where they could hold him would turn

a large force against Sedgwick and probably overpower and cut him to pieces[.]

And at daylight about 1 corps of the enemy came in from our left and in less than 15 minutes from the hour we discovered them occupied their old works and were in front of us and in rear of Gen. Sedgwick, who was about 4 miles beyond their works. Thus I waited like a spectator at a public execution for I knew they would attack Sedgwick and overpower him by a superior force from all sides.

I stated this, but most of my fellow officers thought Sedgwick had made [unclear] with Hooker, but I knew better and I prophesied an attack on him at 4 o'clock and at 4 o'clock they ridiculed my idea by saying "It is 4 o'clock, and no attack has been made yet."

I replied "I hope there won't be, but there is time enough to cut him in pieces yet," and in less than 15 minutes they attacked and this single corps fought till after dark and fell back towards the river above [unclear] away from us after about much speculation being indulged as to the results, most all very hopeful, I told them Sedgwick was cut to pieces and gone at them a battery of artillery opened up river with heavy and rapid fire pounding a position that Sedgwick had occupied in the day and almost all agreed that it was Sedgwick shelling the rebels but I told them that Sedgwick was attempting to cross the river and the rebels were shelling the crossing, and I was right[.] But from some cause[.] I think because the enemy underestimated his force or allayed this attack to late his loss through a great misfortune was not so severe as I had expected, but as [unclear] is known. But to sum up all[,] we have been whipped twice in this place and this last time in a manner disgraceful to the commander and to the country. And all the bolstering politicians or [unclear] papers can't make anything else of it[.] I should like to comment upon the plan or at least the most reasonable interpretation of his movements but I have not the time[.] I only write to tell you I am alive[.]

But I will tell you what changed my opinion of Gen. Hooker[.] That some one had the kindness to send me a Daily Tribune containing his testimony before the War Committee, and it satisfied me that he was a braggart and his only hope of success before the public was [unclear] And as for truth, I would not believe him under oath after his testimony for I never read anything so unjust, unreasonable, false, and egotistical as that testimony[.] And I tell you such a man is not to be trusted even if he had the ability[.] And he that is so wise in his own concept and sits in judgment with so little scruples and hesitation upon them must certainly never have thought of the doubtful questions that arise to a candid mind[.] I tell you if he wins, which he may do, it will be because his army wins in spite of him[.]

All I can hope is that in all these trials, God may not forget them, for I see no other hope[.]

As ever your son, John Ball

✳ ✳ ✳

Camp near Falmouth, Va.
May 24th, 1863 Sunrise

Dear Father,

Your letter as also the diary came duly to hand and I take this opportunity to write a few lines. I have been officer of the guard[.] Yesterday I took the cool of the morning for this purpose[.] The heat here is excessive[.] Yesterday seemed like Harrison's [unclear] I am sorry to hear that Antoinette is sick[.] I certainly hope it will not continue long[.] Agnes has not written me yet—

You speak with some warmth of the manner in which the newspapers excite and deceive the people[.] I did not see any other prospect for them and anticipated it.

I will accompany this letter by some papers[.]

We are doing at the present time nothing more than the Guard Fatigue and police duty and some way with this they keep us well employed[.] All the 9 months and 2 year regiments are gone or going home[.]

9 months men I would not I would not give a penny for a million[.] That is time to make a man but it takes longer to make a soldier[.] (entro nous)

We had one Regt of them in our division[.] The first battle was antietam[.] As soon as they came under the artillery fire they scatered against orders behind a little hill and woods and were ordered back to reorganize at Fredericksburg[.] 1st they were driven from their position on picket, every one of them, by a few shells and scattered everywhere and did not get their colors again till a week afterwards and at the last battle their time was nearly out and they said they were not going in if they could help it and they broke and ran at the 1st shot of artillery and came near breaking through our line for we were marching in the second line and directly behind them but we brought them up standing[.] Such is my experience with nine months men[.]

I know that there may [be] good Regt now organized but they are better for [unclear.]

What do you think of the arrest and trial and imprisonment of Valandingham[?] I understand there is much feeling by men of all parties upon the subject[.]

What do the people say about Hooker and Halleck[?] What do you think of the decision of the sect of war on the $300 clause of the conscript act[?] That I think will make the opponents of the war take some action[.]

I received a letter from Edd Thompson a few days since[.] I am not pleased with the photograph of myself which you received by Mr. Winslow[.] I received a letter from Mr. Winslow containing a copy[.]

I see I have filled my sheet and you must realize that I do not frequently write a little before breakfast[.] And it requires an early answer[.]

John Ball

✽ ✽ ✽

Camp near Falmouth, Va.
June 13, 1863

Dear Parents,

I wrote you several days since informing you of the probable of the army[.] Although we have been frequently notified to hold ourselves in readiness to march and some portion of the army have moved, we are yet in the same place[.] But I would now inform you that from appearances it is almost certain that we shall move within the next 24 hours[.] As I understand matters, I approve of the move at least a move, and in the direction that this now seems to take[.] I only think it should have been six months earlier[.]

I write now to inform you and also to enclose an ambrotype of a group of my Brother Officers together with my present Col. Colvile[.] You see he is in his drea..., i.e. a loose, Brown linen coat[.] I'd asked him for his picture and he consented. I prefer him in this negligee, for it is himself. In personal he is a monster. You can judge of his height in comparison with mine. But like the stories of Mark Rose, I would say.

The representation in the picture is nothing compared to what he is when he straightens himself (which he sometimes does height.) 6'4" in his stockings. A capacity for aleing and drinking that has not been known since the days of Maximilian. A faithful follower of Rip Van Winkle and David Crockett. I did not say much about him when I was at home, but I had so much else to speak of. But if I ever have leisure, I would write his biography. I may be obliged to take a dose of pills to keep down amity/civily, but they will help me to analyze his character.

The picture on the extreme left is my second H. Bruce. The other is my jolly friend Gertrich Blood, but enough of the native American [unclear] to [deny is crossed out, as well as denny] (how do you spell it) denye it. Do you not emulate the independence and resolution of the man who has the fortitude to spell McGmis Maginnis.

Well I would not have this prejudice you in regard to my esteemed friend for he is a worthy fellow, but he has this one failing. If he had only had a little more foresight and been born in Amerika that would have almost unexceptionable.

But love to all. Good bye.

Wm P. Ball John Ball

✳ ✳ ✳

On the March
Sundown, June 17, 1863

Dear Parents,

I have a letter in my valise which I had written from Fredericksburg the day before our departure, but could not send you because the mails were stopped[.] And as I have stocked my haversack with some blank letter and as this is the first time I have opened it since I started, I thought I would write. I am now waiting for some supper when it is said we shall resume our march, but we cannot march far for the men and officers are nearly dead[.] Ours was the lot to be the last regiment to leave Fredericksburg and we have now arrived on the north side of the Occoquan 7 miles from Fairfax Station[.] And tis said we are to march there to night, but I fear the division cannot be got them[.] My [unclear] the very hardy are one great burning, aching stone bruis[.]

The dust today has been terrible, and some of the way almost equal to our march from Harrison's Landing. But the march was not as severe because not so long. But no army in America has marched with its [unclear] as the 2nd corps[.] The 6th corps precluded us the same [unclear.] Our regiment marched our 3/2 miles and was then ordered and went back 1 mile below Fredericksburg and occupied a new picket line for about one hour and started at day light yesterday morning[.] I am in excellent health or I could not have stood this march[.] I have seen many fall in spasm from heat and exertion and I suppose we have lost hundreds who were not able to come through[.] And the ambulances were not sufficient[.]

But I judge from what I hear that they may come in some time within the next few days[.]

I saw several cases of sun stroke and heard of many more in [unclear.] Medical Director of the corps said he had [illegible—written in fading, smudged pencil] anything and call to my duty [unclear] and if I hope to see a more favorable [unclear.] I shall be out in [unclear.] I can do something effectual[.] You have doubtful heard that the enemy is in Pennsylvania[.]

John Ball

✳ ✳ ✳

Camp [unclear], Md.
July 16th, 1863

Dear Parents,

I wrote you from the Battlefield of Gettysburg. Did you get my letter? Sent it by a citizen a courier. [unclear] And I now write a few words today. I am safe and well. The enemy escaped us but he suffered much in the movement and may suffer more yet in consequence. But I am glad we did not assault him in his position for it was a very strong one. But he divideth, constructed a bridge at a place and time. Gen Meade* did not. I think if it was known to be possible his retreat might have been made more disastrous. I will also take this opportunity to send a letter and ambro type which I wrote to send from Falmouth but could not on account of suspension of the mails and has been in my valise since until today. I should write a longer letter but to-day is the first day of rest since I left Falmouth and all administration business seems to be pressing and still we are to keep 3 days cooked rations in the haversack. I suppose we will march about the day after tomorrow. I received your letter and Agnes' at Frederick. I have not had the time or opportunity to write many whom I had expected to [unclear.] I shall expect to hear from you soon.

> *John Ball*
> *Capt. 1st Minn. Vol.*
> *P.S. I forgot to tell you that I am a Captain*
> *John Ball*

✳ ✳ ✳

Rutland, July 23/63

Dear Son,

We received yours of the 5th after the great Battle at Gettysburg not till the 16th and also the one with the pictures of your brother officers last night the 22[nd.] It seemed a great while after the battle before we got yours of the 5th but still we had not much reason to expect one for after reading the description of the First Minnesota in The Tribune we thought you must be one of the number this time certainly that had gone down, for it did not seem possible that you could escape[.] And to think that you should be one of the two that should escape uninjured seems a miracle[.] But you better believe there was a rejoicing when we got your letter relieving us of the anxiety and suspense, we was in for a few days for everyone I met the first word was "Have you got a letter from John[?] Have you heard from John[?] I saw Uncle Samuel Payne[.] He had read the same in the paper that we had but he said he would bet you would come out all right, said you had been through so many battles and came through all sound—would this time[.] I saw Orvin Hill just after I got the letter[.] Told him you was all right[.] He gave one of his funny laughs. Said he guess you are bullet proof[.] He had read the same in the paper and thought your chance was small to come out sound[.]

Now a little about myself[.] I am not able to do any thing[.] The boys are out haying. Sam [is] here looking out of the window[.] George is here to work helping them[.] I am … discouraged[.] It is five weeks since I been able to do any thing but milk some of the time[.] Not able even to do that as they say it is nothing but a lame back[.] Your mother's health is not as good this summer as usual. Still she keeps sound about her work[.]

You speak of the New York riot as though they was hired by government[.] Now I would like to know what you mean by the government, whether it is the General government or the government of the State of New York[.] I claim it is the Papperhads resisting the draft and I think Governor Seymor is at the bottom of it for I heard a man from New York say that if Seymor told the boys not [to] resist, they would not[.] It would be just as he said[.] I think it [is] just so for he went there and called them his friends in his speech[.] As to the justness of the conscription bill, I hardly know what to say[.] Perhaps I am not a judge[.] Some don't like the $300, [unclear] and some does[.] I think there is more that can pay now than if it was left out for they can now pay $300, but if it was left for each one to get his own substitute, they would run up very high out of the reach of the common people[.] George complains very much thinks the $300 claim is wrong[.] George does not say much to me but I suppose he is quite pappery the rest of the family is old women and all[.]

Nett got her letter last night[.] George brought it over this morning[.] You spoke in her letter about marching for a month[.] [unclear] It has been very warm here and I suppose still warmer where you are[.] You speak as though when your time is out that you enlisted for if you lived to see that time you should be out of the pay[.] Well I blame you[.] Oh I hope you will be spared till that time and come home and not be obliged to leave in one short week[.]

As to your brother officers, please give my respects to them all, especially to your little Col. Colvill. He would be such a one as I would like[.] I could get behind him in time of battle to keep off the hail stone[.]

You spoke of Col. Colvill being wounded at the last battle[.] I hope not seriously[.] If there is any change in your Division Commanders or Corps Commanders, write us[.] Say in your next what date your Capt. Commission is[.]

From your Father, W. P. Ball

P.S. If you could get your photograph taken with your uniform and sword large enough to frame and send it, if you could we would like it. I don't know if you could[.]

✳ ✳ ✳

Baltimore
Aug. 7, 1863
Capt. John Ball,

Dear Sir:

We received this morning your favor of the 3ʳᵈ inst. saying you gave to Mr. Rufus King about the 3ʳᵈ May last year to pay for the suit of clothes you order of us for Lieut. Bruce. We have not received the money from Mr. King; or heard from him in regard to it.

Glad to hear from you again and hope you escaped at Gettysburg without a scratch.

Very Respectfully,
Hopkins Eichman

✳ ✳ ✳

Gettysburg August 18
Capt Ball

Dear Sir

I received a letter from Lieut. Bruce the 1ˢᵗ of Aug in answer to a letter I had written to in reference to any mail that I might have in the Company; he states that he made inquiry of Sergt Wright and found that I had but two letters and that Sergt Wright had given them to Sergt Childs that Childs acknowledged that he had received but had thrown them away on account of there being encumbersome on him and threw them away without looking at or opening them[.] now Capt I think that on the day that the Regt left here Childs was at the Hospital and I told him that I was expecting money from home and that I wanted he should tell Sergt Wright so and have him keep my mail until I could send for it. now I cannot immagine why Sergt Childs should get my letters to take care of then throw them away without opening or asking someone to take them, surely one or two letters was not much weight and I know that anyone would have done as small a favor as that; To assure you that I was expecting money and that it was sent the Col proposes that [I] send you my sisters letter that I received since[.]

I hope that Sergt Childs will make this satisfactory.

The Col is doing well at present [.] Will the detail that I sent answer; Parker is in the General Hospital[.]

You will find enclosed a line from the Col[.] Ollie King has been here and some Minnesotians[.]

My kindest regards to Lieut Bruce and men[.]

From your obediently
Milton L Bevans

✳ ✳ ✳

Camp 1ˢᵗ Minn. Vol. Inftry
Robinsons Ford Rapidian River, Va
Sept. 22ⁿᵈ, 1863

Dear Father,

Your letter and also one from Agnes came to hand the day before yesterday at this place[.] You were too fast in congratulating yourself that I was not far from you for since I left the Peninsula. I have not been so distant from you. We suddenly received marching orders on the fifth at Brooklyn only one hour after I sent my last letter to Agnes. My Regt embarked next day Sunday the 5th, and I remained over two days and joined them at Alexandria on the 8th and on the 12th marched for the army on 14th to arrived at Gen. Meades Hd Qts. were ordered to move on and join our old corps which was in advance at Culpeper.* Joined them at Culpeper on the 16th. The next day had a skirmish with the enemy and drove him beyond the Rapidan* [river] where he had taken up a strong position. The 19th marched to this ford and have since been engaged in picket duty and occasional skirmishes. So instead of being in the delightful society of Brooklyn we are in the [unclear] front occupying the most remote bend of the river which forms over present front of operations. And instead of comodious tents and the comforts which we had prepared for a rest, we have not seen a bit of our baggage until today and have passed through the Equinox storms without tents or blankets. But I am in good health and I hasten to write you this [unclear] for we shall probably march within 24 hours for wet or under orders and have to carry 8 days rations and there have been cannonading on the right all day. So I suppose there is to be a fight or footrace pretty soon and perhaps both.

So you need not be surprised if you do not hear from me soon, but do not borrow any trouble on my account.

Regards to all the friends and love to all the family.
John Ball
Capt. 1st Minnesota Vols

✳ ✳ ✳

New York
Sept. 25, 1863
Capt. John Ball,
1st Minn.

Dear Friend, I received your note of the 22nd with one enclosed for my cousin which will be duly forwarded.

You must excuse me for not writing to you before but I have been so very busy that I have not had time to write to anyone.

One of the little boys has received two letters from a member of your regt. So that I have heard from you indirectly.

Seems that Rosincrans has been united in Georgia from the accounts we have received, although I hope it may be a mere rumor.

I have heard through the papers of your advance and sincerely hope it may be successful.

The Brooklyn folks remain in "status quo"—nothing more in New York arrival of a fleet of Russian steamers, eight in all, they look quite formidable. My Uncle's folks all wish to be remembered to you. They are enjoying their usual good health. I have been quite unwell for a day or two, and am still under the weather. You will please excuse the shortness of this note as I am quite busy and believe me to remain your true friend.

Joseph T. Welwood

✳ ✳ ✳

New York
Oct. 5th, 1863

My Dear Friend,

Your favor of Sept. 30 and Oct. 2nd at hand. I have been out of town for a day or two, and did not get them until this morning.

The commission you gave me to procure you an "Ahn's Textbook of the German Language," I was unable to fulfill. I went to the publishers of the work, and was informed that the book was out of print, and they had no copies on hand. I tried several other places, German book stores [unclear] but could not procure one, for which I am very sorry. If there is any other book or article that I can procure you, I would do so with pleasure. I enclose the money you sent.

I am glad to hear that you are in your usual health and spirits, and am happy to state that I have entirely recovered my own health. Most persons do suppose that I am a very healthy person. I presume it is because that I am large and heavy looking, and with the exception of the rummatizm, to which I am subject, I am quite healthy. Anything further occurs from indigestion as I am very irregular in my habits of life, which causes all this. I have tried to reform but find it almost impossible. I have succeeded in a measure, but not wholly.

I see by the papers and your letter that you have not advanced any lately, which is not a matter of surprise, since the check we received in Georgia for by all accounts it was not a defeat, in fact the rebels acknowledge a defeat, or something just as bad.

There is nothing I would like more than to go through a campaign. I think it would improve my health, but I am afraid it would have an opposite effect on my manners.

But whether it would or not, I would like to try it, if I could only get an appointment as aid de camp on some general's staff, I would like it very much. But I am afraid that I can't get anything of the kind, so I must be content as I am. My prospects in business are improving and think I would be better off to stay where I am, although if I was offered anything of the kind I think I would be tempted to accept it. I thought I was competent.

I have been down the island on a visit to my Father last week and have had a splendid time, came down this morning. I do not board at my uncles now. I left there two or three weeks ago. But I believe they are all well. I have not seen any of them since your last letter. I delivered your note to cousin Mary and she expressed herself very much pleased.

I would like very much to go up to the lakes hunting or fishing with you. I am very fond of both amusements. I am a better fisherman than a gunner. I suppose there must be plenty of game in that neighborhood at this time of the year.

I will obey your requests as soon as possible in presenting your respects to my uncle's family, hoping you will excuse haste and chirography I remain[.]

Truly Your Friend,
Joseph T. Welwood

If there is any other commission I can execute for you, do not hesitate to ask it, and I hope I may meet with better success than here to fore.

To Capt. John Ball

❋ ❋ ❋

Oct. 12, /63

Dear Brother,

Your letter of the 22nd came to hand on the 30th and found me at Antoinette's. I was there making a visit as my school did not keep. Father came up in the morning to see about some butter and brought the letter up to me. Nette and George were home Sunday. They were well as usual. Burt is getting to be quite a boy. My school is going off finely. We have about 23 scholars. The teacher boards to our house from Friday night till Monday morning, and she is full of fun. I can tell you, next Saturday we are going to have the horse and carriage and go over to the Middle Road and call on all the folks.

We went to church Sunday and Aunt Frany was quite sick, so Mother stayed all night with her. She came home [unclear] morning and Aunt F. was some better. They thought she would have a run of the fever, but Mother thinks she will get along now. Also Mrs. Gustavne Champlain has been quite sick, but is getting better.

You spoke about Dora's getting your letter. I saw her a week ago Sunday, but I did not think to ask her. Well as it is time for me to retire, I will close to tonight.

Well Sunday night has come, and I will try and finish my letter. Mother has gone up to see Mrs. Champlain and Father has gone to school meeting. Melissa and myself are all alone this evening, but I expect she will go away soon for she is expecting to go to a party at Mr. Henry Monroe's, so when she goes away I shall be all alone.

Mother wants me [to] tell you that she thinks you rather imprudent corresponding with a Lady of so short acquaintance. I heard tonight that Henry Payne was home on a furlow. I believe he is going to stay a week. Father received a letter from Henry Andrews last week.

He was well as usual. As I have lessons to get, I will close. Write soon.

John Ball   From Agnes Ball

✳ ✳ ✳

Head Quarters 1ˢᵗ Minn. Vol
Camp Near Warrenton, Va.
October 29, 1863

My Dear Captain,

Your kind [unclear] of the 21ˢᵗ first just came to hand. I am much pleased to hear from you and hope that your wounds may not prove so dangerous as they are represented.

Your valice, haversack, revolver, field glass, and sword I turned over to the quarter master with instructions to forward them the first opportunity, but am informed by him that he "just" could not get a chance to send them. The cars will be up tomorrow and I will see that you get all your baggage. I wish you would have someone to write often giving me the state of your health. We have all been very uneasy about you but hope that you may soon be restored to your former strength. All the officers join me in kind regards to you. You will hear from the regiment very often.

Your most oldest servant,

Markis Downie

Capt. John Ball 1ˢᵗ Minn. Vol.

✳ ✳ ✳

Camp 1st Minnesota
[unclear] Warenton
Oct. 29

My Dear Ball,

I did not hear that you were wounded until you were taken from the field—and did not see you. The first news we have had of your whereabouts—was [unclear] up by Oscar King—just now [unclear] here. I need not assure you how deeply I [unclear] indeed the whole regiment sympathize with you and how sincerely we wish for your recovery. Which I trust may occur as soon as possible. As we all feel continually anxious—please advise us of your state of health as often as you conveniently can. We are all well, and in camp no movement seems contemplated at present. Though of course we can not tell what a day may bring forth. I got a short note from Colvill last night. He heard of your wound—and wished to know how and where you were. Indeed that was the purpose of this letter. He only said in [unclear] to himself that he was better—and hoped to go home soon.

Truly your friend,
Martin McGinnis

✳ ✳ ✳

Watertown
Oct. 29th /63

Friend John,

Your father came into the store this morning just after I came from breakfast and I assure you I was glad to hear of your condition and above all to know that you are in good hands and doing well. I have thought about you much since I heard of your being wounded and have been extremely anxious to know how badly you are wounded and whether you were having good care. And I was very glad to hear exactly how you are. Let us be thankful that your life has been spared when you came so very near death.

Your father says you are abundantly able to <u>read</u> letters—but in poor condition to write answers. So we will not expect answers for the present. If my poor letters will help you to forget your troubles for a few minutes I shall be abundantly paid for writing.

I hope you will improve rapidly and that we shall soon see you [unclear] us again to recruit your health— and visit your friends—in fact, I think you have done your [unclear] and ought to <u>retire</u>—I don't know of a Regt that has done any more <u>hard</u> service than the Minn. 1ˢᵗ and it is hard to think of shattered ranks and see what they have sacrificed to support our glorious republic. I am thankful the people are encouraging their soldiers with their votes and that public sentiment has so rapidly changed within the past year. Every state so far has shown by the result of their elections that Copperheadism is fast [unclear] and loyalty rising to sustain the administration in the hour of its need. This state you will hear from soon and you may depend upon it— Seymor and his clique will get a rebuke that will get them to thinking. You will hardly believe me when I tell you that democracy has sunk so low in this town. That with all the greatest guns they can get here they [unclear] fill Appalo Hall—they have made several efforts—bands of music [unclear] and have made a perfect <u>puzzle</u> every time. On the contrary—the Union meetings are crowded to overflowing—and Washington Hall will not begin to hold the crowds that turn out to every meeting. It has got to be a decided disgrace to be known as a democrat in this town. And they sneak around with as little noise as possible. Seymore's name is a byword and cursed by almost everyone. We will show you what New York will do to the Copperheads. In a few days people are getting their eyes opened to their foul purposes and saw that they were drifting to other distractions of Country. Your friends and acquaintances are all very anxious about you and one rejoiced to hear that you are in a way to recover. I don't [unclear] of any news of interest to re-tell—unless it be of Mrs. Hopkins, who is in Middlebury Corner—very sick and we are very fearful she will not recover. I will write again in two or three days.

Thompson

✳ ✳ ✳

Hed Qrs 1ˢᵗ Minn. Vols.
Camp n. Warrentown
Nov. 4ᵗʰ, 1863

My Dear Captain,

You must think indeed very strange of me not to have heard for so long a time neither of your effects nor of myself.

When I left you at Centreville, my intentions were first to send immediately your carpet bag to Adams Express office in Washington, but as I came to camp it seemed as if we were falling back towards Alexandria and supposing you might stay there, I concluded you would get it sooner, but instead of moving back [unclear] and we moved forward the next day and were the whole time some distance from any rail communication. Your *letter announcing your stay at Mansion House Hospital [unclear] reached me both together at Auburn on the 22ⁿᵈ October. I tried every day by going at corps division and brigade headquarters to find a chance to send your articles, but could not find it possible, there being no through connections to Alexandria and officers going there went on horseback so that I could not send through them.*

A few days ago Marble, our former hospital steward, went to Washington and he agreed to take some of your thing[s], saying that if he had to stay 4 days in Alexandria to find you, he would do it. But I went to bring him the things in the evening he was gone already. On my way there I met Oscar King just coming in; he could not take them. I myself had made application 10-12 ago to go to Alexandria on important business for the regiment, no answer yet.

Segt. Wood is now temporarily with Capt. Johnes, he is going every day to the depot (the [unclear] yesterday here) and sees if he can meet somebody who can be entrusted with the baggage.

Your revolver, sword, belt, carpet bag, and haversack, also glass, are in my possession.

Rest assured that I did everything that could be done to send your things as early as possible; I might have done better to send from Fairfax the first day to Washington if I had not thought we would get there ourselves. Now I hope that you get well as soon as you can. If I get to Alexandria or if any of our men should come, we will not fair to see you.

Colvill is at Chataqua County, N.Y. doing well. Adams at Hastings expects to rejoin the regiment soon. Peller had last week a resection of the arm bone but is doing extremely well. He is at Baltimore, 19ᵗʰ Monument Square.

Here all are well except Maj. Downie, who has a stiff neck from a boile.

Our boys built a nice log camp, but we are expecting to move every day. I suppose our gens want to find Mr. Bob Lee, from whom there is no news in camp for some time. Our regiment don't reenlist at present they want first to be at liberty a little while.

The 7th, 9th, and 10th Regts of our state have left and will join Gen. Sanborn's in southwest Missouri. I believe now my dear friend, let me urge you again to get well as soon as possible, which with your happy temperament and good constitution, I hope to God, won't be long. Let us hear occasionally. I for myself promise to write you oftener than I have done at present.

With my best wishes I remain,
Truly Your Friend,
Francis Baasen

Capt. John Ball
1st Minn. Vols.

✳ ✳ ✳

Hd Qs 1st Minnesota Vols
Camp Near Brandy Station, Va.
November 17/63

Capt John Ball, 1st Minnesota Vols., has permit to remove from the government warehouse in Alexandria or Washington all his private effects.

To Whom it May Concern: Francis Baasen, 1st Lieut.
Approved. Quart. Master 1st Minnesota

George W. Holmes Capt.

✳ ✳ ✳

Watertown, Nov 4/63

Friend John,

My two or three days have stretched out to four or five—but I have had things to look after that I did not expect so soon at least. Mrs. Hopkins died at Middlebury Conn. Last Saturday morning—her family except Martha were all there to come home with her body—but did not all reach there till after her death. So I had my hands full to make arrangements to receive them. They arrived at 10 o'clock yesterday morning—had funeral services at the house at 3 o'clock—the sermon will be preached next Sabbath. What terrible afflictions we are called upon to mourn within a short length of time—six deaths within the family as you may say within as many months—war does not equal this. It is a true saying that "in life we are in the midst of death"—we are continually admonished that this life is short and uncertain and that we have little time to trifle with—it takes some of us a long time to <u>realize</u> the object for which we are placed here and to improve our opportunities as we ought—There is so much in this world to draw our minds aside, that we almost forget our purpose here and were it not that death is continually staring us in the face, we should almost forget our duties—and obligations to our creator.

Well we have gone through with another election campaign and from all I can learn my predictions in my first letter are correct—it is estimated by knowing ones that we and 30,000 ahead in the state—our Copperhead friends gnash their teeth in despair—for they see the "writing on the wall" in respect to presidential prospects—Of course Union men feel glorious, and well they may—there is hope for the nation yet—last fall it looked black as night to Union men—to see such a man as Seymour elected for the express purpose of throwing blacks under the wheels of government to give the south easy advantage in their power. But thank God the people are turning the old <u>European State</u> back into her loyal position to take her place once more to crush out treason. I wish I could know how you are getting along—but I shall [unclear] you and getting better unless I hear to the contrary.

There is no news that I know of—I have not seen your father since he returned from you. The weather is mild for this time of year—we have had no snow yet—which is a great improvement on last year—I will write again in a few days.

Your friend, Thompson

I see Daniel Eames is home for 15 days.

✻ ✻ ✻

George W. [unclear] Capt.
P Asst 2. M. U.S. Vols. 1st Brigade 2nd Divis. 2nd Corps.
Camp 1st Minn. Vols near Brandy Station, Va.
Dec. 11th
Capt. John Ball,

Dear Sir,

I have commenced as many as six (if not more) letters to within the last week. This evening I received yours of Dec. 4th and I will answer it before I go to bed. I would like to give you a detailed account of our movements for the last two weeks, but you know I am a poor hand, and can get the outline of the operations of the Army in the papers. Our Regt for a wonder came back without losing a man, but I can answer you we were in some very difficult situations. We crossed the Rapidian on the 26th at Germania Ford. The next day we moved south towards

Orange Court House. We met the rebels on the Turnpike Road leading from Orange C. H. to Fredericksburg after quite a skirmish we drew them back to their first line of fortifications. The 2ⁿᵈ corps was now formed in line of battle, the 2ⁿᵈ divi on the right. The 15ᵗʰ Mass. was sent out as skirmishers and were driven out of a [unclear] of woods they tried to gain. Our Regt was now called on. We moved up in line of battle expecting every moment to receive a volly when we had arrived to within 200 yards of the woods, Company H was sent out in advance and moved up on the Double Quick to make a short stay of it, no enemy was to be found we remained there for the night, the next morning the hole corps was found in line by divi front 2ⁿᵈ divi leading. We marched forward expecting to storm the fortifications in real earnest the rebels had in the meantime fell back to their main works two miles. We moved up to within a mile of them and laid out on picket that night. The next morning our corps, the 3ʳᵈ, and one divi of the 6ᵗʰ moved to the left of our line two miles. The order, I have since learned, was to storm the works by eight o'clock the next morning, we was in position. Our Regt Deployed as Skirmishes in front of the brigade by two o'clock in the morning (I don't know what kind of weather you're having in New York, but it was extremely cold) with [unclear] we was not allowed to have any fire and all we could do was to walk round and fancy what a time we was going to have in the morning in front of a storming Party. Well, daylight came at last and for the first time we could see our position. You can fancy a hill about five hundred feet high with a slope of 35 Dig the rebels on top and you at the foot a clear open field. We could see them as plain as (I was going to say as we could at Fredericksburg but that is no comparison).

If we had stormed the works by daylight perhaps we could have [unclear] them. But as soon as they Discovered us they was hurrying to and fro troops passing Batterys getting in position by ten o'clock they had as large a force as we had and 24 Cannon to sweep that hill while we did not have a cannon that could be got in position. The day wore away. Officers would look up the hill and then at each other shake their heads and ask if the [unclear] of storming the works had not been given up.

All day long we lay in plain sight of them and they of us not more than eight hundred yards apart, and hardly a shot was fired. They I suppose was waiting for us to attack, and I am quite sure a good many of us was waiting for night. That night soon after Dark we left and the next day was on the north side of the Rapidian we came back to our old camp, but only stayed a few days and then moved out here about a mile to the front. The boys have put up good. [unclear] Lieut. May and myself live together we have a comfortable House. Our camp is about three miles south of Brandy Station. I suppose you know Capt. Burger has resigned and left ours. They have commenced to grant furloughs. I could get one if I wanted it but I shall not go at present. We expect Col. Adams here tomorrow. There is not news I will tell Sergt. Wright and have those papers sent you. Parker came back and he is cooking for me. All [unclear] respects.

You have not seen Col. Colvill yet I suppose. I will not write any more tonight. If you can read this you will do well.

From your friend H. Bruce

✳ ✳ ✳

Camp near Brandy Station, Pa.
Dec. 21st/63
Capt. Ball

Dear Sir,

Some weeks since I sent to you for the transfer papers of property, which I am [unclear] owing to the want of those papers tis emposibel for me to make my returns. We are required to [unclear] returns of camp and garrison equipage. Should like to have all my accounts settled by the first of the New Year. I was notified unless I made my reports my pay would be stopped till my returns was made after the Battle of Bristow, we were for some days before we had any opportunity of getting our papers with [unclear] to you and could not have an inventory of the property taken and presumed wood have no difficulty in regards to getting the transfer made. I thought [unclear] of gone to the hospital but was informed you were able to move round and help yourself in a great many respects. I came to the conclusion as soon as able you would send me all the papers I required.

Lieutenant Bruce informed me 10 days since you would forward them the first of the week. Please attend to this matter. By doing so you will confer a great favor on me.

Let me know how your wounds are doing. Col Adams is with the Rigt all [unclear] in front.

I remain yours truly,
Thomas Sinclair

Left to right: Lt. Col. John Ball, Col. James Gilfillan,
Surgeon Henry McMahon, and Maj. Martin Maginnis,
members of the same regiment in Gallatin, Tenn.

Reconstruction and Post War

Despite his severe injuries, John returned to duty on January 19, 1864. The First Minnesota Regiment was mustered out 3-½ months later on May 5, 1864, but it wasn't until April 9, 1865, that General Robert E. Lee surrendered and effectively ended the war.

In addition to the severe wound to his groin, the attack at Bristoe Station resulted in a bullet passing through John's arm and another hitting his field glass. It's unclear whether it was the right or left arm, but the wounds left him unable to write for a period of time.

John reenlisted as a second lieutenant in the Second Minnesota Battery in May of 1864, according to the May 28, 1864, Winona Daily Republican. However, there is no military record that he actually served in the battery.

He apparently went to New York in August, where he was reassigned as a major and then lieutenant colonel in command of the 11th Minnesota in Gallatin, Tennessee. Brigadier Alex S. Webb wrote the letter of recommendation for lieutenant colonel. An 1853 graduate of West Point, Webb was awarded the Medal of Honor for gallantry and heroism at Gettysburg. John's superior officer, Col. J. B. Gilfillan, who became Chief Justice of the Minnesota Supreme Court in 1969, was called away often. This effectively put John in command of the regiment in Gallatin, Tennessee, an assignment that he describes as being on a "peace footing."

Most of the 1864 packet contains sympathy letters and news from friends and family. The tone of the letters has understandably changed again—to lively banter and talk of checkers, ice skating, and billiards. There are updates on military details, land deals, deaths, marriages, and amusing thoughts on courting ladies in New York.

"If you will take the advice of a fool 'beware of all old maids,' writes his good friend I. T. Welwood. "When you chose a wife get a good natured one. It is not my place to give advice to my superior which I think you had better give me some."

In another jovial letter, Welwood freely advises John on how he should spend his post-war days: "I shall be pleased to hear from you, and rejoice at your success both in love, and in arms. Hoping that you may obtain a speedy promotion, and that your valuable life may be spared to the close of this war, and longer, so that you may have the pleasure of helping to repopulate the depopulated parts of the country."

John passed up the New York ladies to marry a hometown Minnesota girl on Dec. 27, 1865: Emma C. Lewton of Winona. Born in Louisville, Kentucky., in 1840, Emma was the daughter of Martha Parker of New York and James T. Lewton of Bristol, England. John and Emma met in Winona, and in the next 10 years, they had three children before John died of consumption in 1875: Mary A. (b. March 12, 1867), William Parker (b. June 7, 1869), and Charles Goddang (b. Aug. 23, 1871). Mary was eight years old when her father died, and she eventually married Morris Peter Hanson on condition that his mother-in-law, Emma, live with them for the remainder of her years.

There are indications that William and Charles may have been in the custody of someone other than their mother for a period of time until the 1890s. The two sons eventually struck out on their own as adventurers. William was only six years old when John passed away, and he eventually sought his fortune in the Klondike gold rush in the Yukon Territory some-time around age 30. Charles was merely four years old at his father's death. He ventured to the Congo, where he worked for King Leopold of Belgium and created his own packet of letters and a historic set of knives used by the native people of the Congo. He eventually died there of dysentery. Emma outlived her husband by 60 years, dying on Feb. 17, 1936, at age 96.

In addition to his marriage to Emma, the 1864-1869 letters highlight three other significant events: John's promotion to lieutenant colonel in command of the 11th Minnesota by Gov. Stephen Miller on Sept. 7, 1864; his reconstruction era "peace footing" in Gallatin; his election to the Minnesota legislature.

John was known in Winona as Colonel Ball, and there are thousands of newspaper references to his political activities, home, wife, and the John Ball Post of the Grand Army of the Republic. One of the most intriguing events in John's life during those years has to do with a fascinating letter written by Governor Miller at the end of 1864 indicating that slanderous accusations made against them both had been laid to rest. The letter is torn, and it's unclear what those accusations were and who made them. However, one can conclude that they may have been politically motivated.

> "1. If as I supposed there was no truth in the charges, I thought it best that there should be no notice of the matter upon the official records of the Department.
>
> And 2. I thought that your enemies and mine were giving the matter so much importance that it required an authoritative contradiction in some shape.
>
> [Letter torn and illegible] contradiction has come with such emphasis from Maj. Maginnis that I trust it has vindicated both of _us_, and placed a final [unclear] to the slander.
>
> Believe me to be Very Truly Your Friend
> S. Miller"

The accusations against both men may have stemmed from sour grapes over John's recent and rapid promotions, first to major in August and then to lieutenant colonel in command a month later by Governor Miller. A search through the Winona Daily Republican database found the following explanations and defenses of John from an article in the Saint Paul Press dated Nov. 23, 1864, which references accusations made in an anonymous letter sent to the newspaper:

"A soldier of the Eleventh regiment writes to a friend at Faribault a bitter complaint against Lieut. Col. John Ball, who is accused of not only having been a supporter of McClellan for the Presidency, but is also charged with having ordered the runaway negro servant of a rebel woman to be delivered to her; and further, with having refused to heed the entreaty of a colored man who invoked his protection in behalf of a son who had been cruelly treated by a rebel master. In the last named case, Col. Ball is reputed as having said in reply to the invocation of the aged negro: "Go along! I have nothing to do with it;" and the account proceeds to say, with a sneer remarked: "I am not issuing emancipation proclamations." These statements will sound somewhat strangely in the ears of those who have known Lieut. Col. Ball during the past six or seven years. That he was a partisan of Gen. McClellan—passive, however, rather than active—in the recent campaign, is an admitted fact. But as to the allegations contained in the letter referred to, we think there must be at least another version of them. They are certainly not in keeping with the antecedents of John Ball, who is so well and favorably known in this community. We prefer to believe that Col. Ball is not deserving of the indignant epithets hurled at him through the St. Paul Press by a correspondent at Faribault, at least until we shall have received more reliable and convincing evidence of his guilt than that produced by an anonymous letter-writer, whose forte appears to consist chiefly in rant and vulgarity."

Those accusations against John prompted comments from newspapers throughout the state. The Red Wing Republican, edited by Col. Colvill, provided the following response shortly thereafter:

"After a long and intimate acquaintance with Colonel Ball, we presume we know something of his sentiments; also did Gov. Miller at the time he appointed him. Col. Ball was never a Democrat. He was an original Republican, and warmly in favor of the Emancipation Proclamation from the beginning. This we know, and consider the Press as very ill advised and hasty in thus traducing an able and brave officer, who has fought and bled and done his whole duty for his country in the field, while the editor of the above sheet has, we hope done his whole duty, and manifested his patriotism and made his living with ease and safety at home."

The St. Cloud Democrat weighed in similarly:

"It has been our privilege and pleasure to number Col. Ball, during the past six years, as one of our warm personal friends. We have always considered him a high-toned gentleman, and far above prostituting his position as a military commander into that of a slave-catcher. We believed him a good soldier, and worthy the responsible post he occupies. And we hope and believe that we shall yet be able to contradict on the authority of Col. Ball himself, the above statement."

Tennessee at the time of reconstruction in 1864 was leading the southern states with significant change. No southern state was allowed to rejoin the Union until they ratified the 14th amendment, and Tennessee was the only one at that time to accept the amendment. John was in a challenging position as the leader of a regiment sent to aide reconstruction. In general, he found the people of Tennessee open and amenable to change when some 4 million freed slaves were given citizenship and the guarantee of equal rights under the law. Most could not read or write; they were extremely poor; few had homes.

Emancipation created a chaotic state where former slaves faced severe conditions, disease, and death. Commanders often were at a loss as to how to deal with the large numbers of former slaves in need of basic essentials. One of the most interesting letters in the collection, written from

Gallatin to his parents on May 2, 1865, describes some of the challenges of reconstruction:

>*"I am surprised at their willingness to make the best of what they probably <u>think</u> a bad matter[.] On several occasions lately ladies have acknowledged to me a change of heart on the subject[.] And you can readily conceive the situation when women <u>acknowledge</u> a <u>change</u>[.] They['d] speak freely of their abhorance of the Yanks when they first came But now they don't see so much to abhor[.] Some say there is no difference between the two people[.] They frequently cite incidents of young ladies who once spit on the Yankees and declared they would never speak to one have since married one[.]"*

No record or letter could be found depicting John as harsh or aggressive in his post in Tennessee. His regiment apparently has a good reputation, as indicated in a Sept. 4, 1866, letter written to John from T. Barry: "The announcement that a man belonged to the 11th Minnesota would be a perfect passport all through Tennessee."

John's letters indicate that he had a peaceful and hopeful approach to reconciliation and show that he was at times an eloquent writer. In the same letter to his parents, he reflects on the death of President Lincoln:

>*"I know you have mourned over the death of President Lincoln[.] It seemed as if that act was the last poisonous drop left in the expiring reptile[.]And whether the victim was the man that History will pronounce him or not it is a great blow to the people who had selected him as the representative of their wishes[.]And one that will recoil upon the instigations in the unrelenting vengeance of future years[.]"*

His letters indicate that in the early years of the war, John was a Republican. But after the removal of Major General McClellan by Abraham

Lincoln in 1862, John voted for Democratic Party Candidate McClellan in the 1864 presidential election. When he ran for the position of Winona County Auditor in 1866, he ran on the Democratic ticket, sparking outrage from the formerly supportive Winona Daily Republican, which on Oct. 31, 1866, stated:

> "The candidate for County Auditor on the Mongrel Ticket, when commanding a portion of the Minnesota Eleventh regiment in Tennessee, got up a reputation for herding secesh [slang for secessionist] chickens, very much to the annoyance of his soldiers. He has now taken to calling the muster-roll of the Democratic fowls in Winona county. There will be a flutter in that brood one of these days, and their keeper won't be able to protect them. The sharpest shots will come from the "boys in blue" who were compelled to do hen-coop service at John's bidding in Tennessee.... John will get rolled in on election day at a rate of speed that will astonish him. He will then realize what it is to be a foot Ball, and get kicked.... Col. John Ball, having been infected with the "virus" of Johnsonism, is doing what he can, as the hermaphrodite candidate for County Auditor, to resurrect the Democratic party of this country. "No use doctorin,' " said a Hoosier veterinary surgeon to a crowd who had gathered around a sick horse; "no use doctorin' that ere animal—his eyes is sot!" John's McClellan medicine won't help the unfortunate Democracy a particle. Their "eyes is sot."

Ironically, it would appear that after the war, John was neither a card-carrying Democrat nor Republican—he acted more like an Independent. A "fence-sitter" in the latter half of the 1800s was called a mug wump, with their mug on one side of the fence and their wump (rump) on the other. An editorial that appeared in the Winona Daily Republican on Nov. 1, 1866, questioned John's vacillation between the two parties:

"It is a fact that Col. John Ball, who is now the candidate for the County Auditor on the Mongrel Ticket, nominated by Johnson men and Copperheads—is it a fact, we ask, that this Col. John Ball is the same Col. John Ball that sought the nomination for Register of Deeds on the Republican ticket not many weeks ago? If this is so—and the statement is made to us upon very good authority—then does it not seriously compromise Col. John Ball's consistency and honor that he should have so suddenly changed his position for the purpose of obtaining a petty office? But possibly Col. Ball may have been wrongly accused in this matter. Will he say so over his own signature? We call upon him to deny the charge, if he can."

The Winona Daily Republican wrote a lengthy, scathing attack on John's character on Nov. 3, 1866—the day before the election. He lost the following day to his Republican opponent by 32 votes in a tight race.

"Col. Ball's Copperhead organ whines piteously because we have during the past week thrust some pretty "sharp sticks" at him. Can't help it. He deserves it. When the colonel was in the field, in Tennessee, and was accused of having too much sympathy for rebel widows and compelling his brave boys to do guard duty over rebel hen-coops, we for a long time resisted the accusations, and through our columns did what we could to preserve his fair fame, under the belief that he was unjustly aspersed. Facts are stubborn things, though, and can't easily be put down. Col. Ball not only brought the hen-coop reputation back to Minnesota with him, but has contrived by his political maneuvers since his return, to impress more deeply upon the public mind the character which his own men, whether justly or unjustly, attributed to him in Tennessee. Two years ago, Colonel Ball opposed Abraham Lincoln for President, and voted for McClellan. This was his privilege, and no one objected. A year ago, Col. Ball voluntarily acted as a delegate in the

Republican State Convention, and supported for Governor in that Convention, Wm. R. Marshall, who is well known as one of the most Radical Republicans in the State. This, also, was Col. Ball's right and privilege to do, and no one objected. At the next following election, however, Col. Ball voted against the ticket which he helped to nominate. This year, his own name was freely used as a probable candidate for Register of Deeds on the Republican ticket, with his knowledge and consent. Failing of success in that quarter, he is now a willing candidate on the Mongrel Copperhead and Johnson ticket for the office of County Auditor. All these things it was Col. Ball's undisputed privilege to do. We do not question his privilege to "swing around the circle" to his heart's content. It injures nobody—affects nobody for either good or evil, except Col. John Ball himself. We do say, notwithstanding, that such frequent changes of base argue an instability of purpose—a lack of independence—and a disregard for principle—which do not recommend Col. John Ball to the support of the earnest voters of Winona county. These changes demonstrate him to be a weak man in every element of a straightforward and independent character, and they proclaim his unfitness for any office in which stability and self-control are necessary qualifications. The voters of Winona county respect Col. Ball for his services in the army, but the fact that he was a soldier does not and cannot atone for his moral and political weakness and inconsistency, nor does it carry with it the conclusion that he is a suitable candidate for a responsible office like that of County Auditor. Col. Ball will realize this on next Tuesday night if he does not now."

Two years later, John Ball gained the support of the voters and proved the Winona Daily Republican's allegations questionable. He was elected on the Republican ticket to represent his district in the Minnesota House of Representatives. He also was nominated for Speaker of the House, which he lost to his opponent. After one term, he chose not run again, probably due to failing health and a busy household with two young children and a third on the way. But he held other offices: In his later years he served as the City Council School Director, Clerk of the Board of Education, Deputy County Treasurer, County Treasurer, and Secretary of the Democratic County Senatorial Convention. He was a mason, a member of the Soldiers' Orphans' Home Association, and President of the Regimental Association, which among other activities was involved in erecting a monument at Gettysburg. He held these positions while running an abstract business. "John Ball Post, G.A.R., was named in his honor, and indicated the high regard in which he was held by his army comrades," according to the "Portrait and Biographical Record of Winona County."

His health was in decline, and in 1875, he left his wife and children behind in Winona to travel back to Rutland by train to spend his final days on the family homestead. He was described as so feeble from consumption that he needed assistance when reaching the train station in Watertown, New York. He was confined to his bed and died two weeks later on Sept. 29, 1875, in Rutland, NY. His body was returned to Winona by train, and he is buried there at Woodlawn Cemetery.

His parents lived in the house for the remainder of their lives. When they died, Antoinette and her husband (Hickox) moved into the house, followed by sister Agnes and her husband (Johnson) until the 1950s.

The last letter in the collection is written by Antoinette to John's widow, Emma, on Sept. 27, 1876. While it would appear that John and Antoinette never corresponded, there was an exchange of letters between the two women after his death.

"My Dear Sister,

Very glad indeed was I to hear from you to learn of your safe arrival at your home in good health and good spirits wish I might say but I thought of you so much and have pictured to myself so many times how lovely you would be & how I should feel and have imagined it so keenly that it seemed as if the burden of grief would almost overpower you. But as our day is so shall our strength be. And time moves on just the same whether

we are bowed with grief or full of gladness. And we know
as the time draws near that calls us to our friends."

John was clearly loved and appreciated by many in Winona, as his death records show. The Bar Association called him "one of its most valued members ... feeling that in him were happily combined all those qualities which make the good citizen, the valuable friend, the true man." The Board of County Commissioners characterized their relationship with him as "unbroken harmony and by sincere admiration on our part of the ability and honesty with which he filled his important station."

His obituary in the Jefferson County Journal stands as a testament to a life of sacrifice and courageous contributions during one of the most difficult times in US history.

"Death of a Brave Man—Col. John Ball of Winona, Minn, who has been home on a visit to his father, Wm. P. Ball, and has been lying at home hopelessly sick of consumption and brain disease, died on Sunday last in his 40th [sic 39th] year.

Col. Ball emigrated to Minnesota in 1853, where in the practice of his business of surveying, he became well acquainted with both the topography and people of his adopted State and other parts of the North-west, which was then largely inhabited by wild Indians. When the rebellion broke out he assisted to raise the first regiment from his State, enlisted himself as a private. When the regiment was organized, he was made a sergeant. His regiment was one of the first in the field, and like our own 94th NY, had the fortune to be in a large number of hard-fought battles. Col. Ball was engaged with his regiment at the first and second battles of Bull Run, the battles on the Chickahominy, at Antietam, and Gettysburg and many others, twenty-two in all. He was severely wounded at Bristow Station, and disabled for some time. He was noted for ability, coolness and bravery, and was early promoted to captaincy. As an example of his obstinate bravery when under fire, it is related of him that at one time when obliged by the rebels to retreat, he emptied his revolver at them and then threw it in the face of the nearest one. At Gettysburg his regiment suffered severely, eight times the colors were shot down, but each time they came up again and were brought safely off the field. The commissioned officers were all killed or disabled except two, Capt. Ball being one of the two, the command of the little remnant of the brave old regiment devolving on him for a short time. Re-enlisting at the expiration of his term of service, he was sent to Tennessee, where with a guard under his command, he acted as provost marshal until the close of the war. Upon his return home, he was sent to the Legislature of his State, serving his constitute with ability and integrity—Refusing to serve a second term he applied himself closely to his private business for some years, finding time however to assist in building up the beautiful city in which he resided. He was some time since elected treasurer of Winona County, which position he occupied at the time of his death. His life was no doubt shortened by overwork of body and brain, his untiring industry showing him no rest. When obliged by ill health to stop all work, thinking a change of air would be beneficial he started East to visit once more the home and loved ones of his childhood. Failing rapidly on the way, he reached his father's house only to die. Thus another of Jefferson county's honored sons has passed away, one of whom we may well be proud, and one of the many noble boys, who by their own native ability, industry and perseverance work their way up from obscurity to high positions of honor and usefulness."

—Jefferson County Journal, Sept. 29, 1875

The 1864 Letters

War Department
Provost Marshal General's Office
Washington, D.C.
Jany 21ˢᵗ, 1864

Dear Captain,

I regret exceedingly that I did not see you again (as I intended) before you went to the front.

I have just rec'd another letter from a brother-in-law of the late Capt Farrell requesting me to use every exertion in finding his (Capt. Farrells) trunk and clothes etc. I think you informed me last fall that a Capt. ____ (I have forgotten the name) had some part if not all of the Capt. things in a trunk. If possible please see this Capt. & if he has anything that belongs to the late Capt. Farrell send them to me at this City. I think if you mark them to my address, the Adams Express man at the station will receive them.

Please do what you can in this matter & write me at your earliest convenience.

I regret that I could not have gone to the front with you.

Give my regards to Capt. Duffy & others of the Regt.
Your Obedient Servt.
L. B. Gillet
Provost Marshal Gnl's Office
War Department
Washington, D.C.

Capt. John Ball
1ˢᵗ Minn. Vols.
Wash. D.C.

❋ ❋ ❋

Mansion House
Alexandria, Va
Feby 27ᵗʰ /64

Capt. Ball Dear Sir

This evening finds me fulfilling my promise to write you though at a later period than I intended when you left here for St. Paul[.] I have been very busy the most of the time since last I saw you[.] I have not played but a few games of checkers since I played with you but I think if you were here I could show you how to play a game and not get any kings. I would like to have the pleasure of trying it to prove the statement. My patients are all going finely there has been near 5 inches of bone take[n] out of the Frenchmans leg he is doing well now[.] I have not heard from [unclear] yet & perhaps never shall[.] I

104

reced a letter from Charles Colerman the other day he is
so he can get round now on his crutches[.]

Mrs. Wright has just been in my room and says remember her to the Captain (with his whiskers) perhaps
if she knew how I have obeyed her orders she would be
[unclear] cuffing my ears to end the joke[.] I don't think
of any news to write that will be interesting to you so I
will wind up my health is good and I am in good spirits
(not whiskey) but feel well in general[.] I will close by wish-
ing you success & hoping this will find you well & that I
may soon hear from you. I am very respectfully your
Obet Srvt
Floyd Ashley.

P.S. Please give my compliments to Pitkin and excuse
mistake

❋ ❋ ❋

*March 1st, 1864
Red Wing, Minn

Captain John Ball

I have got your Sword all right. Col is getting along
very well gaining some. I am going up to St. Paul Saturday,
nothing new here, how is it with you Old Billards & Chess
any other game you play. Write please.
H Bruce

❋ ❋ ❋

New York
March 8ᵗʰ, 1864

Friend Ball,

Your letter dated Winona Feb. 27ᵗʰ was duly received. I was much pleased to hear from you. I suppose you are having a grand time <u>recruiting</u>.

I have been so much engaged with business for some time past, that I have not had time to write to any of my friends, and hope you will excuse me for my seeming neglect. I have left my former place of business Eastman & Co and am with a new firm, Mis Norton Slaughter & Co in the Cotton & Tobacco trade, and as they are very busy, I work nearly <u>all night, never</u> getting home before eleven oclock P.M. but I don't think I will be so much longer. I receive a better salary and have a more congenial position, with a good prospect ahead.

Things remain in <u>"status quo" uptown</u> I have neither <u>advanced</u> nor <u>receded</u> and am still in a state of single blessedness. I advertise for a wife occasionally, but the last time, I have not been able to answer any of the letters I received. The previous advertisement I answered several letters, one lady in particular I corresponded with for three or four months, exchanged pictures, and finally met her. She was quite a fine looking girl and repectable, but now I shall have to drop it, as I have no time to spare. I still manage to call upon two or three ladies but don't feel inclined to come <u>up</u> to the <u>scratch</u> yet.

We have had some splendid skating and I have never before has such an excellent time. I <u>never</u> took a lady out there but <u>always</u> had one after getting there, and that you know is all the fun.

I am very much obliged to you for your kind wishes and advice with regard to visiting my uncles family, but am sorry that I cannot act upon them. I do not wish to go where I am not wanted, by all the members of the family, and while they or <u>some</u> of them believe that I gamble and frequent houses of <u>ill fame</u>, I <u>never will</u> go there and I think the charges are to <u>absurd</u> to attempt to <u>disprove.</u> I am not ashamed nor afraid for anyone to know what I do or where I go, all my dealings are open and above board, but that's enough on that subject. I shall be pleased to hear from you, and rejoice at your success both in <u>love,</u> and in <u>arms</u>. Hoping that you may obtain a speedy promotion, and that your valuable life may be spared to the close of this war, and longer, so that you may have the <u>pleasure</u> of <u>helping</u> to repopulate the depopulated parts of the country.

I am truly Your Friend
I.T. Welwood

❋ ❋ ❋

Merchants Hotel
St. Paul, Minn.
May 24, 1864
Lieutenant —

I shall embark for the front Thursday the 25th instant. You will be in readiness to join me at Winona with such of the mean as may be in that place awaiting my arrival. I do not know at what hour the boat will leave. Therefore cannot tell what time we shall be most likely to reach Winona.
Yours & [unclear]
W. A. Hotchkiss
Capt. Comd of Mins. [unclear]

John Ball
2 Lieut. 2 Min. Vtrs.

✳ ✳ ✳

Winona, June 17, 64

My Dear Friend

Your short epistle from Nashville was recd while I
was at St. P—on a short spree. When I returned I noticed
with interest what you mentioned—and can easily imagine that your orders were not such as would be most welcome to a veteran from the Potomac yet doubtless better
things are in store for you. So cheer up—read a chapter
in Regulations which [is] what you would do were you
only omnipotent—buckle on your [unclear] and travel.
I return to you the only letter that has been recd
by me as yet it has not been necessary to send any to
Brooklyn.
You know that a very negligent manner is sometimes
[unclear], as well in correspondence as otherwise.
The 6th Regt [unclear] down yesterday for Arkansas.
Weather [unclear] hot and dry. Nothing new that I re-
member, only our folks have all gone east and left me a
lone widower, Bachelor or something.
Write me often [unclear] me.
Sincerely your friend
John Sherman

✳ ✳ ✳

U.S. Hotel July 12th 1864

John Ball Esq

Sir If you are anxious to go to Washington immediately you will have an opportunity of doing so tomorrow. Call at the [unclear] fair grounds as early as possible tomorrow morning and inquire for Lt. Carmichael Commanding 13th Company. I can assure you an opportunity of going along now it won't cost you anything. I would also like to have you along as I want to borrow your sword. I have got no sword and the stores are closed so I cannot buy one. If you can arrange it so as to go along with us or let me take your sword along it will be a grait accommodation to me. Please call and see me at the [unclear] fair grounds as early as possible tomorrow morning and you will much oblige your friend.

Thomas Charmichael
1st Lt. Co H 37 Wis Vol

❋ ❋ ❋

Brooklyn July 20th, 1864

Friend Ball,

I received your kind note and was glad to hear you was among the Living. I am in good health as all the family are which I hope you are enjoying when I went home from my business they told me I had a letter from Washington and when I opened it I could not read it fast enough to let them know you was well. Business is very dull there is not much doing in any kind of Business there is 2 & 3 Regiments now fitting out for the [unclear] one in particular enlisted about 300 boys in it. But when it was getting mustered in they threw out all the boys and sent the men to Fort Richmond Statin Island. What position do you now hold in your Regt and how long do you intend to serve[?] I did think I would try a soldiers life but then my folks when I told them did not like the idea. I was offered a Color Sargt. position if I would go but the folks did not see it.

When you write to me again please be so kind as to let me know the name of that Young Lady you send letters to up town New York. I was told last week you had fallen in love with a Young Lady up town. But if you will take the advice of a fool "beware of all old maids." When you chose a wife get a good natured one. It is not my place to give advice to my superior which I think you had better give me some. If you should come to the City do not forget our house. It is at your Liberty. My head is full of any thing else but writing a good letter. Excuse me in writing about your Sweet Heart, but you had might to know what kind of a person I am. All the folks send their Love[.] Mine also[.] Write soon and believe me.

Your Obd't Servant,
Thomas A. Wetwood
28 Adelphi St.
Brooklyn

✳ ✳ ✳

Rutland, July 28/64

Dear Son,

Yours of 15th came [to] hand last Sunday the 24th which you better believe relieved our anxiety very much for we had made our minds we should not hear from you again for I expected you would write as soon as you got to the cumberland army and we knew they had some bad fighting there and we had made up our minds that you had fell with many others and your Uncle Henry said he did not believe we would ever hear from you. Well we have and we can't feel glad enough and if you knew our anxiety and feeling you would write oftener than 2 or 3 months if you was where you could.

Well it appears that you have had some trouble since you left home last winter. I should think, rather a discouraging summer's work but hope you will come out all right.

Well I believe that when I last wrote your Mother was sick. Well she has got her health as well as it was before she was sick. As to my self I don't claim to be sick but I have not been able to walk to the barn since last March. I can ride out if they drive the buggy up to the door.

Well we have had the greatest drought here that I ever know it 7 weeks to day since it rained to wet the ground it was very wet in the spring and the grass got a very good start and we shall get a very good crop of hay. But the spring crops are not worth harvesting in may places the boys will finish my haying to day with the exception of getting in 1 or 2 loads.

Daniel Eames is at home very sick it was thought when he first came home he would not live but a short time but I believe he is some better and there is hopes of his getting up again.

Joseph Todd, the man that married Giffy Lewis is dead. Died near Petersburg. He belonged to 10th Artillery.

George & Antoinette are well. Agnes is now playing and singing old [unclear.]

The impending draft makes quite a [unclear] among the Copperhead. They were mad about the $300 [unclear] last year and now they are mad so I don't see as it makes much difference. My will not be suited any way.

Write soon. Yours as well.
W. P. Ball

❊ ❊ ❊

[Almost illegible]
Camp near Petersburg
Aug. 2nd, 1864
Capt. Ball
Dear Sir:
    Your note is received. I have to state that no letters bearing your address have been received. Should [unclear] any come, I will send or [unclear].
    I was glad to hear from you Capt.: but why didn't you tell me something what is going on with you? Can't you offer him to drop me a line explaining of your course since leaving the <u>Blonde Old First</u>.
    Things move on with us [unclear] often: we have had rather a hard time since coming back but what are left of us are all right.
    Capt. Crots is in camp now. Will be on with a stack of goods soon for the [unclear]. Bill Harmon is at Corp Head Quarters was over to see us today. Capt. Heffelfinger is in the <u>Sanitary Business</u>. Calls on us often.
    If convenient with me going [unclear] I should be pleased to hear from you. [unclear]
    Yours Truly,
    E.P. Perkins

❊ ❊ ❊

New York City
August 10th, 1864

Mr. John Ball (late a Captain in the 1st Regiment of the Minnesota Vols.) is well known to us as an efficient officer; and as one in whom I could always have great confidence—
He has been wounded several times and has shown himself to be in action a gallant officer—
I cordially recommend him as worthy of trust and deserving of favor—
Alex S. Webb
Brig. Gen. U.S. Vols.

❊ ❊ ❊

Durand Aug. 12th/64
John Ball Esq.

Sir I take this opportunity to drop you a few lines. I have some very serious notion of volunteering. And if you want any recruits in your battery I should like to join your company. If you will let me know by return mail I think I will join you in a few weeks. Our chances here are rather good to be _Drafted_ and I do not like to run the risk. All well hope this will find you the same. Please answer immediately and Oblige.

Yours Respectfully,
W.P. Lewton

❊ ❊ ❊

State of Minnesota
Executive Department
Saint Paul, Aug. 20, 1864
Capt. John Ball

My Dear Capt.,

I have written and telegraphed to Washington and New York for you several times. If you can report to me in person immediately I will give you one of the field positions of the 11th Regiment Minn. Vols.

Truly Yours,
S. Miller

* * *

Washington D.C.
War Department
Adjutant General's Office
Monday night, Aug. 22nd, 1864

Dear Friend Ball,

I have just got through with three hours writing. I am on duty as the heading of this sheet indicates and as I have found out tonight. Yesterday I remailed you a letter that was post-marked New York. This evening I found a telegram about the Majorship in my box. I will enclose it, though ere it reaches you, I presume you have got the "ship" and under full sail. Look out for snags, and other unpleasant obstacles as you push ahead. It is now ten o'clock and the state of my nerves admonish me to lay aside the pen for the night. Let me hear from you at your earliest convenience. Remember me to Governor

Miller and tell him if he has anything for me to engage in this, the last year of my military career, that he had better send for me. Remember and speak to Gregory about the Alexandria property if you have an opportunity.

> *Hurriedly Yours,*
> *Will Kinkead*
> *Maj. John Ball*
> *Saint Paul, Minn'a.*

✳ ✳ ✳

New York, August 25, 1964

My Dear Major:

I was not a little surprised last Monday morning when a letter was handed me addressed in your familiar style postmarked "New York." I soon made myself acquainted with its contents when my surprise gave way to pleasure: and here Capt. no: excuse me <u>Major.</u> Permit me to sincerely congratulate you which I can the more heartily do knowing that you will fill your new position with satisfaction to your superior officers and honor yourself. I will take advantage of your kind offer to serve me and request you to call upon Chas E. Mayo, Esq. and say to him that I used every effort to find Capt. Farrells trunks but without success. Went to each of the Hotels and examined every thing they had in the way of trunks and in fact done all I could do in the matter. You may also call upon G. G. Griswald, hand him my regards and say that I shall expect to see him when he comes on to purchase his fall stocks, you can give him my address. Let me hear from you soon.

Truely,
L. B. Gillet

I shall be pleased if I can serve you:

✳ ✳ ✳

Head Quarters 11 Minn. Vols.
Camp Miller Minn
Sept. 9ᵗʰ, 1864
Dear Parents

I wrote you from Washington some time since[.]

Since that time I have been called to Minnesota by the Gov to take command of the 11 Minnesota Vol Infty[.]

I am now Lieut Col Commanding [unclear] regiment camped near Fort Snelling Minn[.]

At the time I wrote you I expected to go south to open trade in the insurrectionary districts[.] As I considered my application to be appointed Assistant Adjutant Genl. Had failed but since I have been commissioned Lt Colonel of the 11ᵗʰ I have rec notice that a recommendation had been forwarded to the War Dept which would give me that position I first asked[.]

So you see after a summer poorly spent I receive a windfall of appreciation[.]

I have a full Regt of 1000 men and the material is the best in the state[.]

I expect orders to leave this place for Nashville Tenn— sometime next week

My Col is a stranger to me but he bears a high recomment[.]

He is now in Mississippi and will not probably join us for a month yet[.]

My major was Adjutant of the 1ˢᵗ Regt and my quartermaster was a Captain in the 1st[.]

Several of my line officers were also in the first[.]

I have expected to he[a]r from you my letter via Washington[.]

But I know you will address me now and I shall get it wen if it follows me to Atlanta[.]

Address Let Col John Ball

11ᵗʰ Minnesota Vols

Care of International Hotel

St. Paul Minnesota

Love to all & C

JB—

❊ ❊ ❊

Saint Paul, Dec 12th 1864

<u>Unoffical</u>

Lieut. Col. John Ball

11th Reg't Minn Vols

My Dear Col.

Yours of the 30 [unclear] is just received, and I am fully satisfied of the truth of its contents.

Major Maginnis's letter which I caused to be published in the Press a few days since, covered the whole matter so fully that I will not have yours placed in print unless there be further reason, or you request me to do so.

It has ended just about as I expected: and I addressed you in a [unclear] official way because

1. If as I supposed there was no truth in the charges, I thought it best that there should be no notice of the matter upon the official records of the Department.

117

And 2. I thought that your enemies and mine were giving the matter so much importance that it required an authoritative contradiction in some shape.

[Letter torn] contradiction has come with such emphasis from Maj. Maginnis that I trust it has vindicated both of *us*, and placed a final [unclear] to the slander. Believe me to be

Very Truly
your Friend
S. Miller

The 1865 Letters

No. 346 3rd Street
Washington City D.C.
Sunday, January 1st, 1865

My Dear Ball,

Shortly after my return from Minnesota last November I received your long and interesting letter of October 29th, 1864, and I really feel ashamed of myself for allowing so much time to pass by and your good letter unanswered. On the 21st of October, 1864, I was granted a thirty days leave of absence and made a visit to St. Cloud and other points in Minn. I had a very pleasant visit, and returned feeling much better. Having been absent so long, and having the charge of the room I was in, I found matters a good deal mixed up, and the work weeks behind from the fact of so many clerks having been granted leaves of absence for the purpose of attending the Presidential election. The consequence was that for a long time I had all I could attend to get matters set aright, and the machine placed

119

in good running order, requiring all my time day and night. All private matters had to be set aside, and it was a long time before I commenced to answer the letters of my friends which had accumulated during my absence, and while under such a pressure of work. I will add further that you are not the only friend whom I have so long neglected; if that will make my apology any better, which I fear not. When in Minn. I saw Gregory and all of our friends in St. Cloud. I could not get the least satisfaction concerning the Alexandria property, and I have my doubts about ever coming to any fair settlement. I found that all the sub-divided lands lying between the Miss and Red rivers were in the market. I procured a Land Warrant and secured my claim adjoining Alexandria. I must tell you my old friend that I find that my general health is very seriously affected by the close application required to fill my present position. I am at this writing feeling very badly and it is with some pain that I pen this letter. I am afraid I must quit the AGO in the spring, but what to turn my hand to next is hard for me to determine. I have thought of a number of things which might possibly render me a mode of making a living; and knowing your willingness to lend a helping hand to a falling brother, I am going to intrude so far upon your generosity to ask that you listen to my story and give me your advice. Under the Act of Congress of 1862, the General Land Office has during the past year issued a large amount of this Agricultural College Scrip the different States, and the quantities that there are bankers in New York holding large amounts of the same, and it is selling at about 60. c per acre. Now it has occurred to me that it might make a profitable business of locating this scrip upon lands in Minn. that I am well acquainted with, provided I could get the men holding the scrip to employ me in making locations for them. I wrote a letter some time ago to Thompson Brothers of New York making known to them my wishes. They replied that they "were only dealing in scrip for cash," but referred me to Taylor Brothers, also to Mefs C.V.G. Woodman of that city, saying "with whom I have no doubt you can make arrangements mutually advantageous." Do you know the last named firms? I have not written to them yet, thinking it would be best to wait until I can get your advice upon the subject as well as the best mode to proceed. This is one thing that has presented itself to me, and I will obviously await any thing you may have to offer upon the subject. Another thing is to see that the State of Minn. has located her Agricultural Scrip, and if not, to see if I could not also get it to locate the States that have Government lands within their boundaries must locate the Scrip and cannot sell, like Pa. and NY, Va.

Will Kinkead

✷ ✷ ✷

Head Quarters 11ᵗʰ minn vols Infty
Gallatin Tenn Febr 10ᵗʰ 1865

Dear Parents

I suppose you have concluded to abandon me and count me as a worm out and hopeless or at least an ungrateful son and that it was not worth while to waste any more material in correspondence. But I am sometimes surprised at your delay because I think some spasm of memory will be accompanied by a desire to know if I am an inhabitant of the "vale of tears[.]"

And I desire to have it known that I am still a sojourner on the way and within no very convenient distance of the "Land of Promise[.]" I have also a desire to know that you are all well and happy i[.]e[.] as well as your age and afflictions will allow me to believe[.]

I hope you have not become proud from living in the city[.] If so I would admonish you against its facinations & to let your children play with other peoples' as your used to[.] I have not told you that I have recd no answer to my last, writen about two months since[.]

Of Course you will answer this and tell me all about the family & neighbors & our uncles and cousins and all the pretty girles and prim old maids but more particularly about George & Antoinette & Uncle Henrys people & Grandpapa[.]

I propose to write a letter to Agnes and lecture her upon the subject of filial duty[.] I immagine when she hears such an Idea suggested, she will droop her eyes & turn her head a little to one side and puff up her lips but I cant help it[.] I think she ought to write me letters from you since you are getting old and almost unable to write so long a letter as I want to get occasionally[.]

Ed Thompson also has deserted me (and I think I can guess the cause he has got married or expects to)[.] And I don't know as I can claim a single constant friend in the old Circle. Medora & Allice I am indebted to[.] I promised to write to Allice and neglected it but would now redeam my promise but that I am ashamed[.] Medora wrote me last but soon after I recd her letter I was traveling and very busy for a long while and neglected her until I thought no appology was eafficient and would not attempt to render one[.]

Sometimes when you delay writing I think perhaps something has happened that you think better not to tell me and so defer writing but I will not believe any such thing[.]

I suppose you want me to say something about myself and it is not satisfaction to occupy my time with such commonplace subjects[.] However I am still here Comdy the Regt living easy (too easy) with little to do[.] The health and condition of my Command is satisfactory[.] We are occasionally <u>paroling</u> a [unclear] & taming an honest citizen[.] We had some little squabbles with the enemy when Hood was in front of Nashville, nothing of importance[.]

Trains have not be delayed 12 hours on this 40 miles of Road since I came here[.]   Present my kind regards to all who inquire & let me be

Your Son
John Ball

Mr & Mrs William P Ball
East Rodman
Jeff Co NY
PS. Address   11th Minnesota Vols
Gallatin Tenn

❋ ❋ ❋

Head Quarters 11th Minn vols
Gallatin Tenn March 3rd 1865

Dear Parents

Your letter has at last arrived to assure me that I am not forgotten and to intimate that I pleaded an excuse for not writing[.] But although I am not very punctual I never new but one letter before since I came here and I wrote you about Christmas[.] Your letter contains many things I was pleased to hear that you are living in town and have such a family of old friends[.] You express a wish that I was at home[.] But you "Father forgive them JC" think what a bedlam you would have if I was there[.]

Mother would be lecturing me on my behavior before company[.] Aunt Jeannette would slap my face and call me a [unclear] every time I talked sensible[.] Miss Rogers would steal my cigars and accuse me of playing false at cards[.] Hattie would excommunicate me from the regard of all respectable people if I chanced to intimate that the Savior of Mankind was as sound a political preacher as Henry Ward Beacher[.] And Edd would slap me on the shoulder and tell me I talked like a rebel & if Chanced to take up a newspaper and read the money market that Gold was [unclear] and green backs 50 per cent below[.]

Winslow and I would get along very well only we would have to console each other upon the dullness of such a place[.] So Father dont wish me at home[.] Edd tells me in a letter I read at the same time of yours that Winslow wrote me some time ago[.] I have never recd it[.]

I wrote Agnes soon after I wrote you—ie—on valentine day[.]

Edd says he aint married[.] Please say to him that he ought to be and I think he is very obstinate[.] He will know what it means[.] Or Hattie must find out[.] I am pleased to hear that Grandfather is so young he will be considered an old settler one of these days[.] Are Medora & Alice at home[?] What school does Agnes attend[?]

Is Payne still at Clinton[?] How is Uncle Talcotts people[?] Do they keep Mary P. with them[?]

I am sorry you are so confused but I need not say it but I am sure you must enjoy the time somewhat with such a lively Household[.] I think I would like [unclear.] Do you keep the dog Ponto[?]

I don't want to ask rude questions but I would like to know if mother goes to [unclear] parties if so does she drink sparkling wines or scotch whiskey[?]

Does she also insist on keeping ducks and geese in the yard about the house[?]

On [unclear] this over I think it is rude[.] But mother you know it would be forgery if I did not say something to anoy you.

I am grieved to hear of the death of Charley Eames[.] I was not aware that he had gone to the army[.] Is Henry at home and is Daniel still with his Regt[?]

The death of Mrs Moses Eames must also be a heavy blow to the family[.] Is Moses Eames realy [unclear] financially[?] If so what a doubly great misfortune has befallen the [unclear] Mary[.] I hope she leaves her lot resignedly and may soon receive as she [unclear] the favor of Providence[.]

Is Morris Reed still in the Army[?] Tell me something about him[.] Also Henry Payne[.] I have been usualy well except a slight inconvenience a disease called the consumption[.] A severe cough keeps me awake at night which you know is about the greatest inconvenience I could have Because when I sleep I (usualy) sleep with all posible vigor[.] But don't be alarmed[.] I have no notion of dying of the next 150 years If I can help it[.] I cant afford it till the price of cotton declines[.] Give my love to all[.]

Oh I forgot to speak of my old Friend Sarah Dutton[.] I can scarcely say wheather I was pleased or shocked when I read it[.] Sarah is a most excellent girl or I am no Judge of animals[.] Mr Mack is a very pleasant man and a good business man and as Olanger [unclear]* used to say a "gut provider[.]" But I would congratulate Mr Mack[.] If I could have three wives I would consider myself exceedingly happy to take her for one of them[.]

*Olangar [unclear] is a quaint duch friend of mine[.]

Your Son
John Ball

Mr. and Mrs. William P. Ball
Watertown

❋ ❋ ❋

Mr & Mrs William P Ball Wattertown
Head Quarters 11ᵗʰ Minn. vols Infty
Gallatin, Tenn
May 2nd 1865

Dear Parents,

I have neglected your letter but will now endeavor to make some slight amends[.]

I have got back home and am again in command of my Regt[.]

I have a very beautiful camp and my quarters are really splendid[.] I board with a private family and am on a peace footing[.] I think I realize the condition of the reserves of the British Army who were "never to leave the country except when it was invaded[.]"

Our national situation is more satisfactory to me at the present time than I had hoped to see it within the last 2 years[.]

Rebellion died hard but is dead[.]

I still anticipate troubles in [the] future which may be little better than war[.] But I am encouraged by our recent triumphs to believe that our country may be restored to harmony and prosperity and the [unclear] obstacles be effectually removed[.]

I know you have mourned over the death of President Lincoln[.] It seemed as if that act was the last poisonous drop left in the expiring reptile[.] And whether the victim was the man that History will pronounce him or not it is a great blow to the people who had selected him as the representative of their wishes[.] And one that will recoil upon the instigations in the unrelenting vengeance of future years[.]

The weather here has been warm but for the last few days quite cool[.] Last evening the people feared a frost although we have green gooseberry pie[.]And today we had some ripe strawberries[.]

The generality of the people here seem willing to give up the question[.] And I am surprised at their willingness to make the best of what they probably _think_ a bad matter[.] On several occasions lately ladies have acknowledged to me a change of heart on the subject[.] And you can readily conceive the situation when women _acknowledge_ a _change_[.] They['d] speak freely of their abhorance of the Yanks when they first came[.] But now they don't see so much to abhor[.] Some say there is no difference between the two people[.] They frequently cite incidents of young ladies who once spit on the Yankees and declared they would never speak to one have since married one[.]

I am much inclined to think almost any of them would under favorable circumstances become Mrs Mudvill[.]

Yesterday I related an anecdote to a young lady as follows[.]

An old nigar who formerly lived in Nashville went away to the Rebel army with his master[.] A little while since he was captured and came home[.] Soon after he arrived among his familiar scenes he s[t]ood on a street corner (as he supposed unobserved) and uncovered his old gray [unclear] and was heard soliloquising thus [unclear] dey used to tell us de Yankees neber goin to git dis fur[.] [unclear] God I reckon dey go just wor day want to[.] Now deys a walkin in our streets dey a preachin in our churches dey a libin in our houses[.] dey a ridin in our carriages[.] [unclear] God I reckon dey'l marry all our widows[.]

The young lady with a mixture of pleasure and displeasure hesitatingly saw she thought it our justice that they should[.] But with all these happy indications I am in distress that "Othelo's occupations Gone" I feel like Richard[.]

"And therefore since I cannot prove a lover
"to entertain these fair well spoken days
"I am determined to prove a villain
"And hate the idle pleasures of these days

Don't understand me that I have concluded to become a villain[.] But that I feel as if I would soon have to resort to one or the other of these two pursuits and I am best qualified for the latter[.] In that [I] could undoubtedly succeed in the former—Doubtful—

I will answer Agne's letter in a day or two[.]

Regards to all

Yours & C

John Ball

Lt. Col Com F

11th Minnesota Vols

Mr. and Mrs. Wm P Ball

Watertown NY

❋ ❋ ❋

New York. May 8th 1865

My Dear Col;

I enclose your Brooks Bros recpt for payment of suit clothes, also Adams Ex. Co's receipt for the same. I had the box Insd for $100 for which I paid $2. the freight they marked Free for me on act of my being an old Express man. Hold on to the recp't until you get the box or its value.

I trust the clothes will suit and reach you in due time.

Let me hear whenever I can serve you. Excuse brev-ity. I am too busy to write more.

Yours Truly
L.B. Gillet
240 Broadway
New York

✳ ✳ ✳

Lt Col John Ball
11ᵗʰ Minn Vols
Gallatin
Tenn
Titusville Aug 28/65

Friend John.

Your favor of 23ʳᵈ is rec'd.

I cannot tell you how glad I am to hear from you and to look upon your honest old face once more. John Ball you were always a d-d good fellow and one to rely upon. And I have relied upon you and will. Whether you do in me or not—

About this <u>Abstract</u>. *Take it and do well with it if you can. Work at it a while [unclear] what terms you want to make it profitable. Isn't that best?*

I think it has been kept up pretty well in Dinsmore's hands and your labor in getting up the work will be light.

Now I know but little about real estate up there and cant imagine how much a fair offer would be—& prefer therefore that the propositions should come from you af-ter a fair trial.

You know you have a certain Equitable Claim upon that work for your former services.

There is (And here is the rub) a debt on that property of $1500—$1000 to Dinsmore relatives & 500 to Webster & Lake.

If the W&L debt can be kept easy, the other can. & I will arrange it—

So, then, it remains for you to look over the ground + see whether you can make it pay on any terms if you think you can. We shall deal readily—

If I can be of any service in any way it would give me infinite pleasure to help you. The way your [unclear] is the only one in my control at present.

Oil is slippery & you cant tell much. At present I am doing well I hope to make a large sum of money.

If I should, my weasel skin would be always at your service.

Your friend truly Harry Lester

If you want to write me. Do: I want to hear from you. I have no <u>carte</u> at present.

Should I ever have one taken you should have me.

L

✳ ✳ ✳

Titusville Dec 23/65
John Ball

Dear friend

I did not receive a letter from you at St Louis and would have written you before but for being ignorant of your address.

I am more than pleased with the standing of the Abstract as you represent it. And sincerely trust you may make it a success.

As the work is involved somewhat in a moral obliga-tion to Dinsmnes father for money which was to have been secured upon it. I wish you to state your views of the interest you desire to have in it—tho terms & C tell me also what its income what will be the [unclear] of comple-tion, its value & generally anything that will make me conversant with your views & wishes.

Did you foreclose in your own name or mine or both? What I want is simply this.

You have against me a claim for your services per-formed in the commencement of the work—and a further claim to be dealt with liberally & friendly. This I desire to recognize fully. Fix a bargain between us that seems right and just to you. And we shall be agreed at once.

I am glad you are feeling so well satisfied with your prospects. Your cheerfulness gives me confidence that you will not let all my hard work on the Abstract be lost.

I am getting on pretty well but am a long way from the fortune I expect to make.

The Excitement of this business is good for me however.

Yesterday I closed up a big $300.000 transportation Co. for pumping oil 6 miles over the hills in iron tubes underground upon which I expect to make a good deal of money.

This region is a marvel. You must come [unclear] me sometime and look at it. I will give you a mount and take you through scenes such as you have scarcely dreamed of—

I was in Chicago all of last week & came back to a press of business so that you will excuse my long delay.

With many good wishes for yourself and Mitchell
I am your friend
H C Lester

Please write me as often as your leisure will permit. I am warmly interested in your prospects.

The 1866 Letter

Dear Sir,   *Gallatin Tenn*   *Sept 4th 66*

I was truly glad to hear from you you and your whole Regiment are highly appreciated here[.] The people here have no prejudices against Federal officers. Col. Garret who was a federal officer got as high a vote in this county for Rep as did Col. A R Wynne an out and out Secessionist[.] The people everywhere I have been in 7 counties are penitent and sincerely desire the restoration of Federal Authority[.] I have never known the people more peacable law abiding and religious and the best men in it are the returned <u>Southern soldiers</u>. The charge that any portion of the people desire to reestablish Slavery is an infamous falsehood[.] They have no desire to pay the Rebel debt[.] The people through the whole South are a unit for President Johnson. The Radicals are practical Disunionists. They are a doomed party[.] They could not carry on a free government 5 years. I am a foe to Tyrants and a genuine friend of Liberty[.] I am too old to change. *Nothing but Jackson Democracy can save the country.*

Present me in the kindest terms to Col. Gilfillan Major MacGuinnis and every man of your Regiment. The announcement that a man belonged to the 11th Minnesota would be a perfect passport all through Tennessee. May God always bless every man of yours.

Yours Truly

Col. Ball T Barry

NB I enclose you a short synopsis. T Barry

The 1867 Letters

Helena, M.S.
June 8, 67

 *Not hearing from my previous letters my dear col,
I think I'll be gone again—see that you will at least let
me know whether or not you are in the land of the living—if you still are where this will reach you—& if you
are dead—may the lord have mercy on your soul—& "he
arise" on the sins you committed in the body[.]*

 *I have found as you indicated this a pretty rough
country—have worked like the dickens—and am behind
the lighthouse all the time—shot [unclear] when some
strikes are made here—But you see the Lord does not
know where their country is yet—& everything goes by
luck—& mine has been none of the best[.] But really Col.
I struck this country at a bad time—nearly all the [un-
clear] mines were worked out and no new ones of any
richness have been discovered & of I have made no money[.] I am blessed with the idea that the most of my worthy countrymen and fellow patriots are in the same pie[.]*

Still there is a great deal of [unclear] going on—& a good deal of money being taken out here the ground—the [unclear] ground you know—is all taken up and newly worked out—& one has to pay as much to dig into a [unclear] as he can take out of it in a year[.]

The country was overrun last year—Lawyers, Doctors, merchants—Everybody came out too plentiful—there was not work enough—in a [unclear] country so limited—most of them put in a year prospecting for new mines & many have returned to California & the States—[unclear].

There are riches enough however in the quartz lodes of this territory to make a rich state—that will require large amounts of outside capital [unclear] & capital after the Colorado & Nevada excitements is very suspicious of [unclear] investments & the country will be developed it slowly.

I think I shall make for home this fall. I intend to put in the summer and give the thing a fair trial—[unclear] give of the boys that started with me from [unclear] have started to return this morn via Benton & the [unclear] river.

Barber & Webb are here have made no money—but hold some pretty good quartz property—if it ever gets to be worth anything to sell—they [unclear] no [unclear] to develop it of course.

I should like much to hear from you Col.—& hope to hear of your prosperity—& the health of your self and your family. Once I [unclear] you I shall write you more fully & with the best wishes I remain your friend

Martin Maginnis

❋ ❋ ❋

Rochester 9 Aug /67
Col John Ball

Dr Sir

    I have just returned to this place from below on a prospecting tour—Am pleased at what I saw and heard. Thinking that as a matter of course Gov. Marshall would get Winona County to support his recommendation, if fight was made, & considering the short time in which it could be seconds. And the imperfect understanding of the people of Gov. Marshalls connection with the board measure, I concluded not to go near your place—nor have I corresponded with any one there upon the subject. The thought occurs to me now that perhaps some of the delegates, when posted upon the acts of our present State Administration would be induced to give in the [unclear] who are now inclining to vote down this bill with its authors and supporters. Suppose you consult Beech of the Post Office, also Mitchel and others whom you may think it safe to talk with upon the subject. And see if some of the delegates can not be induced to vote against Marshall and the balance of the "[unclear.]"
    I shall be in St Paul on Monday and hope soon to hear from you.

    Very truly yours
    C.D. Gilfillan

✳ ✳ ✳

Simpson & Wilson
Attorneys at Law, and Real Estate Agents,
Winona, Minn
Jany 10th 1869

Col. John Ball

Dear Sir. Send us a copy of each of the State Officers Reports if you can conveniently do so and ablige. If any important bills are introduced & ordered printed enclose us a copy of the same if not too much trouble.
Nothing new here so far as I know.
I guess I will have to constitute myself a Com tee to look after your wife & baby while you are gone Col.
Very Respily Your's
Geo. P. Wilson
My kind regards to any of my old friends who may inquire for me
G.P.W.

The 1868 Letters

Office of Winona Democrat
Mo. 16 East Second St.,
Winona, Minn. Jany 18th, 1868

Hon. John Ball

Dr. Col.—Can you not muster up a little correspondence, and will you not see J.J. Eagan, our telegraphic correspondent, and have him telegraph something every day, even if unimportant? In the absence of regular dispatches, we must make a show of some kind in dispatches and correspondence. Have no time to write much. Highest regards to yourself, Franklin, Hill and my old Ohio friend George. Everything moving right here. Tell Mr. F. his paper is left at house, as requested.
Hastily but truly
Jas J. Mcnew

✺ ✺ ✺

Winona, Jany. 18th 68
Hon. John Ball—

Dear Sir

 I saw by the papers that there is a man by the name of Reed in your branch of the Legislature—whom I believe to be John A. Reed formerly Captain of Co. "B" [unclear] Battallion Minn. Vols—if so he is the man to whom I have written several times for an affadavit in the Pension [unclear] of the Solomon Famham of his Company, but have not been able to hear from him, perhaps he did not [unclear] my letters.
 Now Sir. Will you be kind enough to see this man, and let me know whether or not he is my man. And if he is the man ask him if he will be kind enough to [unclear] the [unclear]—
 Without the [unclear] affadavit we are of a dark [unclear].
 In order to show you—and him—the necessity of this little kindness on his part I enclose you Mrs. Famhams last letter to me.
 Hoping you will be able to render us some assistance in this matter[.]
 I remain
 Respectfully yours
 J.M. Sheardown

❋ ❋ ❋

Feb. 18ᵗʰ, 1868

Schoonmaker, Swart & Drew
State Agents for Johnston' Self Raking Reaper,
And General Dealers in Agricultural Machinery
Col Ball

Dear Sir

  Yours is at home—Mitchel will draft another bill and forward today—I meant as I will—we do not expect the Legislature to do more toward financing the new School building. I did not speak officially in this [unclear] but from the Book—[unclear] and others are of the same opinion—of course the necessary furniture must be furniture of the state, though we have furnished three rooms complete of tuition [unclear] of our citizens over Labour paying [unclear] paid about $2,500.00 tuition [unclear] year.
  Now for a [unclear]
  City has also furnished 3 rooms free of all charges to the state since the organization of the school—I know that some will make all the [unclear] possible—when [unclear] report.
  Yours truly   Wm S. Drew

❋ ❋ ❋

Office of Wallace & Co.
Wholesale Dealers in Dry Goods
New Orleans May 13ᵗʰ 1868
John Ball Esq

Dear Sir

  I wrote you immediately on receipt of your letter of

Apr 20 in relation to the lots—that I would sell for $600—if we thought best-expressing the hope that we would pay sufficient to give your comn [commission] beyond and who make it all [unclear] instead of a [unclear]—but left it with you and [unclear] asked you to make a [unclear] sent to me & I would have it executed—since then I have not heard—I now enclose a letter written some time ago which has been overlooked. Don't know as it applies to the land I now own. It may however. I did own 600 acres some two years ago & think perhaps this letter has reference to that—it has been sold—but it may have referenced to the 400 acres which I now own. Please look to it & report.

    Yours truly
    Ed G. Wilder of Wallace Co.

✳ ✳ ✳

St Cloud, Minn
May 26ᵗʰ 1868
Col John Ball
Winona, Minn.

Dear Sir:

    Will Kinkead died on the 22ⁿᵈ [unclear.] He met death with the [unclear] which becomes a man.

    I saw Hick a few days ago. He told me that I could inform you that it was his [unclear] that Wilson and Emery got form paying Wells.

    From the same conversations I gathered incidentally that he paid $10 per acre for the land.

I had promised Will to get this information for you if possible. I write to fulfill that promise.
Very Sincerely Yours
T. H. Brault

The 1869 Letters

Watertown Febr 7ᵗʰ, 69

Dear Jon

*Well it's a beautiful sabath morning here was pre-
paring to go to church was prevented by an attact of
cholic which I occasionly have rather severe while they
last don't generally last long as it has passed off though
I would participate in answering that very welcome
but long looked for letter and made doubly so by your
assurance that we are going to get one oftener[.] It has
always been an old saying that Children never pay for
their bringing up and as regards dollars and cents perhaps they never do but when darkness of old age begins
to invade us and disease and anxiety obstruct our way
then we feel we have the advantage for the sympathy
and affections of our children we feel of far more value
than dolaars and cts[.] We get rather lonely if some of
them don't come home every week or so[.] Agnes and
Orrin were home yesterday also Uncle Talcolls and Auth*

145

Frony were here[.] All seemed very glad to hear from you[.] Am glad to hear you speak in such high esteem of your wife[.] Feel from what I have herd that you have not over estimated her[.] Orrin came right here told us all about his visit with you felt it was under rather trying circumstances as you were moving yet had first rate visit[.] Brought us little Marys likeness which we think ever so much of but wondered why you did not send the Mothers along to[.] You say you wish I could see Mary you cant wish so any more than I do[.] Can assure you that[.] Oh I do so wish you would come and see us[.] You think I should enjoy the journey[.] Besides I have always had such a desire to see the western country[.] You think Mary is like you that she fears nothing but the dark thing that is more than you feared[.] Can she learn to recite poetry as readily as you used to when I held you in my lap and spun linen[?] Hope she will not be as forward as you was in reading in the English reader[.] Cant see any of your looks in her likeness[.] We had the Children home at Christmas had a tree had a very pleasant time but felt that the presence of you and family would have added very much to our enjoyment the next Christmas[.] If nothing happens we all meet at the farm[.] Hope you and family will be with us[.] Aunt Jenelle health is quite poor[.] She has been with Aunt Frony since last Sept [unclear] Mary Parmalee to get married which took place Jan 5th[.] Her husband is Henry Hopkins[.] They go to housekeeping in about 2 weeks[.] He works his fathers farm[.] Ruth Yendes is teaching school this winter in champion[.] Leady is just the same as ever staid to Uncle J last fryday night[.] Frony said she asked him how Aunt Leady was[.] Said he guessed she enjoyed herself as well as a woman could under her circumstances[.] Aunt Julia was taken lame the same spring that your father was so she is around but is all drawed out of shape with spinal disease[.] Henry pane lives here in town[.] His wife has

got a boy some 3 weeks old[.] Your old schoolteacher Mrs
Johnson is the higher lady teacher in the institute boards
to Mr. Towles[.] She is cousin to Agnes Husband[.] Your
Uncle Henry has just got him a nice prize bey Horses
has just drove by with them thinks they are something
pretty nice[.] The greatest amusement here this winter
is skating[.] They have had one Masquerade and carni-
val at the rink have another next Tuesday evening. E
Thomson goes in costume this time he is still in his gro-
cery and boards to the Woodruff House[.] Mr Eames people are all well for any thing that I know[.] Daniel has
bought the old Warner farm moves on to it this spring[.]
Uncle Calvin and wife start for Troy tomorrow to see
their knew grand son Frank is getting so he can walk
across the house a few words more[.] And I close now[.]
I think you have every reason to think that little Mary
is the smartest little girl that ever lived and presume if
I should see her and get acquainted with her should perhaps think the same but think when you read this poetry
you will feel to [unclear.] We have some smart Children
this side of the Mississippi[.] This Mr Beach was a Brother
of Jenny Eames husband he died last summer[.] Jenny
and Mary were both here last fall staied some four or
five weeks[.] Had a very pleasant time with them[.] Am
very sorry to here of your misfortune but I suppose it's
the dark clouds that make us appreciate the sunshine[.]
Well I will will much love to your wife[.] Accept the same
to yourself[.] Kiss little Mary for me[.] Remain as ever
your affectionate

Mother
Dot Ball
J Ball

❋ ❋ ❋

147

[The next and last letter in the 1869 collection are from Emma Ball's brother, J.L. Lewton, to their father. This indicates that the packet of letters was preserved by his wife, Emma, not by his parents.]

Le Sueur Min June 22/69

Dear Father

I have deferred writing you for some time for several reasons the most important being a scarsity of matters of interest from which to make up anything like a readable letter. Also I had expected some time previous to the recent S.S. meeting in Winona to have been present at that gathering. When I could have seen and talked with you when the time came around the condition of Marys health was such as necessitated my staying at home. There is no day passes that I do not think of and pray for you and I wish it were so that you could come and spend a few weeks with us. the family are as well as usual my own health is poor. I think not so good as usual at this time of year. What an unusual and unpleasant summer we are having. It seems almost as if winter were determined to reign throughout the year. [unclear] grain is promising as well throughout this country as ever before. Corn is rather under the weather. Gardens do not seem to be very prolific only in Potatoe Bugs, of which there is promise of an abundant crop. We have a nice Bed of Strawberries in our yard and expect by this time next week to be luxuriating in Strawberries Cream and green Peas. A number of Sabbath Schools in the vicinity are making preparations for celebrating the 4th or the 3rd of next month, expect to make a speech on the occasion. I hope to be able to get down and see you sometime during the summer but cannot do so unless many matters become easier than at present. give our best love to Mary

& family also to Emma and family. I hope Mary is able to get along with her business matters without any very serious embarrassments. I would like very much to see her. give our best love to Sallie and accept the same for our selves. with our prayers for your present and future welfare.

From your affectionate Son
J. L. Lewton

19 Nassan St. July 18/69
John Ball Esq
Winnona Minn

Dear Sir.

Yours of 11th is recd. I left your note with my friend Col Gillette who tells me he has already notified you where it is. I am glad you are ready to take it up and am needing money. Relative to the business you speak of—I think there is nothing coming to me there. My impression is that Mitchell closed the whole business and sent me some money for the lot. However, if there is anything due me I would be glad of course to have you get it for me. Please see Mitchell and ask him about it[.]

The judgment held against me by Erving aroused from a little game played upon me by young Erving by which I was forced to pay for certain lots in Chutes And Ladders and never got a title to the lots—the [unclear] was for an unpaid balance & I sent the money to Norton who paid the [unclear] & had it [unclear] of record as I presume[.]

If you find that I ought to have anything for the lot let me hear from you[.]

Yours & C
H C Lester

✳ ✳ ✳

Dear Father

I wrote you some weeks ago but do not hear from you in reply. I conclude that you either did not get my let-ter or else did not think it worth while to write one who is so negligent about answering as myself. I write this time to congratulate you on the birth of another grand-son and myself as the happy Father. Theodore [unclear] was two weeks old last Friday morning. Mary & Baby are both doing well he is a handsome boy has a good look-ing head. And I think will do full credit to the Lewton family to which he has the <u>distinguished honor</u> to belong. Rest of the family are all well and we are looking over [unclear] for a visit from <u>Grand pa</u>. I hope we will not be disappointed. shall expect you after harvest at any rate. I intend writing Maxwell to day with reference to your claim to urge it payment as soon as due. if he does not attend to it promptly I would make arrangements to forclose at once. I hope Mary is getting along smoothly with her farm matters and trust that she will be able to make some satisfactory arrangements to get rid of the burden. It must be a great care for her. give her our best love and wishes for her welfare. remember us to Emma Sallie Ball and to all the little nephews & nieces. the time for the assembly of our Annual Conference is near at hand (Oct 11/69) where I will be [unclear] next year. I cannot tell very [unclear] at this same point however. I *am well satisfied that I am in the line of duty and new I in good health could look forward with hope to a successful career. Have you heard from Mother lately[?] Do you know anything of [unclear] circumstances has her ever heard from his [unclear]? I trust he has. We have had a pleasant summer and could never promise better than at present.*

From your affectionate son [J. L. Lewton]

The Ball farmhouse in Rutland, New York, circa 1870.

The 1870 Letters

Winona Minnesota
Apr 3/70

Dear Parents

Two weeks ago I wrote you & gave account of the heavey fall of snow [e]tc[.]

Today there is no snow to be seen except on the north side of the Bluffs and the roads on the prarie & streets of the city are dry[.]The day is a beautiful one but not very warm[.] The ice went out of the river yesterday and one boat came down last evening and went up again this morning[.] No boats from below yet probably tomorrow will bring them[.] The snow did not go suddenly but it has been warm almost every day since I last wrote you— There is some snow in the country yet the frost is out of the ground as soon as the snow is gone[.] Notwithstanding the continued warm and pleasant weather the season is late[.] The opening of navigation and the plowing season are among the latest we have ever experienced[.] Still

153

if the fine weather continues we will soon make up for lost time[.] I have nothing of special news to report—except now I think of it—the death of Old Silsbu whom you thought was once a citizen of Jeff Co. He died very sudenly and did not receive such flatering obituary notices as is usualy bestowed on such prominent characters—The press rather [unclear] at the forlorn condition of his better half who it is said laid him out and came for the coffin herself and seemed to be master of the situation[.]

Among people Generaly—I only heard one standing Joak—going the rounds—That there was doubts wheathe[r] navigation would open at all this spring[.]

[Additional pages missing]

✻ ✻ ✻

June 16th, 1870
Belle-Pluine Iowa

Lieut John Ball

Dr Sir

If you will sign the enclosed certificate you will confer a [unclear], as it will enable me to get my Bounty. I rec. a similar certificate from Lieut Perisem before his Death—which enabled me to get a full Pension which I now receive.

Please signe certif and return to me and you will confer a great favor[.]

✻ ✻ ✻

Rutland Sept 27th/76

My Dear Sister
    Very glad indeed was I to hear from you to learn of your safe arrival at your home in good health and good spirits wish I might say but I thought of you so much and have pictured to myself so many times how lovely you would be & how I should feel and have imagined it so keenly that it seemed as if the burden of grief would almost overpower you. But as our day is so shall our strength be. And time moves on just the same whether we are bowed with grief or full of gladness. And we know as the time draws near that calls us to our friends. Have been to Church this afternoon [.] Mr Hershy had a substitute a young fellow. [unclear] last week we had no rain and the ground was very dry and in some parts people were very much [unclear] to get water for their stock and it has not rained enough yet to raise the streams. Mr Barney met with [unclear] an accident the second day of the fair. As he was coming home there was a number of them that was driving [unclear] fast and he got his carriage ran into and tipped over he was thrown out and his leg broken—just above his ankle both bones were broken & one badly crushed. But came near being with him he rode down with him in the morning. The accident happened a little ways this side of [unclear] Plinny Monroes—so they took him back thru. The doctor thought he would have to stay there two or three weeks.
    I saw Aron, Agnes, and Anne today they were at church so often [unclear.] Anne has been over and enjoyed more than a week with me since you went home. [unclear.] I have not been with them since the Sunday that we was up there with you. Agnes said she looked for us last night but we cant get away very well to be gone overnight.

Ana has been most sick with a cold this past week [unclear] her back is [unclear] lame[.] They have been expecting to hear from Mr. Fellows but have not as yet. [unclear] And there is not a day that there is something said that reminds us of them and you. Give my best love and a good night hug to each of them and reserve a large share for yourself. The boys will work before long.

A H [Antoinette Hickox]

AFTERWORD

Researching Your Relatives
In an Era of Evolving Internet Data

Ancestral research began to change at a rapid pace with the entrance of the personal computer. On a daily basis, new information pops up on the Internet that can broaden your understanding of your ancestors and the time in which they lived. In my own research, which spanned 11 years, I found a wealth of new resources. These included entire books dating back to the late 1800s, old newspaper databases with relevant letters and articles, photographs, evolving family trees, and more. Additionally, I found evolving websites and blog sites where I met people with similar interests who led me to new family "archeological digs."

While compiling information for this book, several people expressed interest in the methods used to obtain a clear picture of John Ball's character and accomplishments. Obviously, the greatest resource was his letters. Family members, historical societies, and fellow researchers also can provide letters, diaries, or information relating to your ancestor. We were fortunate to find a historical researcher who lived in the Ball family house, had neighbors who knew the Ball family, and owned a photograph of the house taken in the 1880s.

There are other common research venues that are standard places to look. Online ancestry databases, such as Archives.com and Ancestry.com, can be excellent sources of information on births, marriages, deaths, military service, social security indexes, and other personal information. Sometimes you can get a free, week-long trial subscription, but eventually you need to pay for their services. Start your research with yourself, then work backward, and remember to explore the branches of siblings and maiden names that can provide new avenues of information.

Historical societies, courthouses, and federal record databases all provide free information about censuses, ancestors, who lived in the household, military records, and even business practices. We obtained useful pension information from the National Archives, which you will find in subsequent pages—affidavits that provided some previously unknown information and a copy of a letter from a hospital that wasn't in the packet that was used to justify a pension for John's widow.

One of our earliest resources that led to valuable information and contacts was a county online genealogical service for New York State. The Jefferson County History Network site had *vast* amounts of useful information relating to where John Ball grew up, such as farming practices, people profiles, census data, cemetery information, and general history for the area. It also provided a list of local historical researchers who were able to hone in on additional information at local libraries, courthouses, and historical societies for a nominal fee. A phone call to the Rutland, New York, Town Hall provided a contact that took photographs of Ball family homes and emailed them to us. Archivists and librarians sometimes know about local sources you might overlook. Try to locate the homes of your ancestors, if they are still standing, and the cemetery where they are buried. Old Bibles were a common place to store information on births and deaths. Obituaries can provide little-known or unknown information.

Reading posts on ancestral blog sites provided links and email addresses for people who had information about family genealogy and the 11th Minnesota Regiment in Tennessee during Reconstruction. These resources led to new information—and friendships. We connected with previously unknown distant relatives from New York and Utah, who had extensive genealogies and family stories. Sometimes your research dovetails with that of others who are writing books, and you can provide or swap information.

Another excellent resource was a newspaper database for Minnesota that began in 1850 and provided a timeline for Civil War articles for Winona,

Minnesota. The Winona Historical Society and Minnesota Historical Society had relevant articles, letters, artifacts, and other historical references. Depending on the era of research, databases can be found in sites such as the Daughters of the American Revolution Genealogy Research System or the Church of Latter Day Saints. We were fortunate to find a historical researcher at The Mary Baker Eddy Library in Boston who had a personal interest in the Civil War and donated countless hours of his time teaching us proper research techniques and pointing us in new directions. Remember to return to libraries and databases because sometimes researchers are loading new information on a regular basis. The Internet's evolving online resources can provide a constant flow of new and updated information.

If your ancestor was a mason, veteran, or member of an organization or religious group, visit that association or church and ask for records relating to when they attended. The Church of Latter Day Saints has gathered extensive amounts of genealogical information about people throughout the world. Reenactment websites are another great resource for those doing military research.

Don't forget to document and check your Internet sources. Are they credible? Some websites provide misinformation to tens of thousands of viewers. Wikipedia, for example, is not always a reliable source. Also, forums and blog sites are notorious for containing inaccurate information.

Finally, try to immerse yourself in the life of the ancestor you are researching. Develop a "relationship" with them, and appreciate their lifestyles and challenges. One of my favorite research projects was walking through the monuments at Gettysburg National Military Park in Pennsylvania, visiting Little Round Top, and watching a Civil War enactment. Museums such as Strawberry Bank in Portsmouth, New Hampshire, or a living history museum are great ways to help you and your family understand and absorb the lives of your ancestors. Such resources will help you develop the inspiration and motivation you need to paint an accurate picture and timeline.

AFFIDAVITS

Martin Maginnis, June 10, 1890,

Helena, Montana

A resident of Helena, State of Montana, Martin Maginnis, being duly sworn, deposes and says that he served from the organization of the First Regiment of Minnesota Volunteers in company with John Ball, of Winona, Minn, whose widow is applicant for a pension.

That I knew said John Ball initially as a Sergeant, 1ˢᵗ & 2ⁿᵈ Lieutenant and as Captain of said 1ˢᵗ Minn Vol Infty. That I messed with him and was his tent mate for a great portion of the years of 62 & 63. That I knew him to be of hardy, robust and enduring constitution. That he was capable of standing and did stand, with less trouble than others, the hard marches and battles in which the regiment was engaged—on the Peninsula, at Antietam, the battles on the Rappahannock and at Gettysburg. That we were both in command of companies on the day of the battle of Bristow Station. The regiment was deployed as skirmishers, for the Second Division of the Second Army Corps, commanded by Gen G K Warren. That we discovered a corps of the enemy endeavoring to advance and cut us off from the ford near Bristoe. That we gave the alarm and engaged the skirmishers of the enemy and held them until the 2ⁿᵈ Division 2nd Corps had time to form a line along the railroad embankment extending from the ford to the cut below Bristow Station. That then in obedience to orders we fell back to the line of battle and that our companies were together. The enemy advanced in several charges upon the line and once seemed about to take the railroad—when among a few others, Capt Ball, sprang in front of the line upon the embankment and firing all the shots from his revolver into the advancing enemy, threw his revolver in their faces. That just as they broke and retreated before our fire, he was shot down, by my side, as we supposed mortally wounded—the ball passing through his groin and carrying away one of his testes. He came very close to death, but unexpectedly recovered and rejoined his regiment, though he never recovered his former vigor and superb health. I served with him until the regiment was reorganized.

In September 1864, we were respectively appointed as Lieut Col & Major of the 11th Minnesota. We again went together to Tennessee. We messed and lived together and were in constant companionship until June 1865 when we were both mustered out.

I distinctly and positively assert that though jealous and active in duty he never recovered from his wound, and that before our parting I felt that his constitution was irretrievably shattered. After this I met him on a number of occasions, at re-unions of the regiment and elsewhere up to the time of his death—and saw a great decline on each meeting—and heard his complaints that he never recovered his health. I believe that his death resulted from disease, induced by his wound and the hardship that he underwent. I repeat that when I first knew him he was in rugged heath and capable of as much endurance and fatigue as any man in the service. He was a brave and gallant soldier, he endured constant service, was tried in many battles and was wounded under circumstances which won the praise of all witnesses. That he never recovered his health, and that his wife and children deserve a pension under the laws.

Martin Maginnis, Helena, Montana, June 10, 1890

C. W. Merritt, September 30, 1890,
Winona County, Minnesota

Personally signed before me the undersigned clerk of said county, C. W. Merritt late a corporal of Co. F, 1ˢᵗ Regt. Minn. Vol. Infty. To me well known as a person of good character & credibility, who being duly sworn upon his oath says:

That he knew the late Lt Col John Ball of the 11ᵗʰ Regt Minn Vols as a Sergt of Co K 1ˢᵗ Regt of Minn Vol Infty. He was in robust health up to the time of the Bat. of Bull Run, July 21ˢᵗ, 1861, when affiant was taken prisoner & did not see said Ball again until Jan, 1863. He was then a Lieut commanding Co F. I thought he was not quite so strong and robust as when I last saw him, but never heard him complain. At the Bat. of Bristow Station he was severely wounded & fell close beside me. I learned from the Surgeon in charge at the time that the ball entered the groin carrying away one of his testes. Contrary to all expectations he recovered & rejoined the Regt. He bore the marks of his severe illness. He was faded & emaciated & complained to me of much pain in the region of the testes. I was detailed as co clerk in making the rolls etc. therefore was intimate with him. He had a severe cough which followed him growing worse at the time of his death, which occurred Sept 16, 1875. Himself & family were frequent visitors at our house, & his declining health was a matter of much concern to all of us. I have no doubt that his disease was caused from his wound and his hardship to exposure incident to the service. I have no interest direct or indirect in the prosecution of this claim.

C. W. Merritt, September 30, 1890, to Chester Halding,
Dept. Clerk of Court, Winona County, Minnesota

James M. Cole, Winona County, Minnesota

I was personally acquainted with the late Lt Col John Ball while he was a resident of the city of Winona, state of Minnesota, both before he enlisted in as a soldier in Co K of the First Reg Minn Vol at the commencement of the War of the Rebellion, and after his return from the army at the close of the war.

Before he enlisted he was in sound health with apparently a good constitution. After his discharge from the army he returned home to the city of Winona in very poor health—much debilitated and suffering from chronic cough with considerable expectoration. His health improved some soon after his return to civil life in 1865. For several years after his health was variable but at no time could it be said that he was in good health. At no time was he free from the chronic cough with exploration which at times was severe.

After he was married I was his family physician during his life and continued my attendance on his family after his death. During these years I made numerous prescriptions for his disability. He was always quite reluctant to take medicine or to follow any prescribed course of treatment, claiming that he was not really an invalid. That the cough would not amount to anything serious for he had it while in the army a long time before he came home.

In April and May 1875 he became so much worse that he was compelled to keep to his bed for several weeks. Until this time he had always perseveringly attended to his business affairs apparently sustained in his efforts by his indomitable will power. After this severe prostration and confinement to his bed he rallied and temporarily improved so that he was able to return to his business office. (He was County Treasurer of Winona County.) But his irritating cough and profuse expectoration with his increasing debility was rapidly wearing away his naturally hardy constitution. Consumption was secure of its victim.

On the 4th of July 1875 he took an active part in the celebration of that day. The weather was intensely hot and he was prostrated by his own exertion while in performance of his assumed duties. From this time he failed steadily. It was about this time that he consulted and received prescriptions from Dr Franklin Staples of the City of Winona, although as I have previously stated he was strongly averse to following the prescribed directions of a physician. He consulted a number of the best physicians in the west: among the number was Dr J H Murphy of St Paul, Minn., in whom he had great confidence in his opinion.

In the spring of 1875 I advised Col Ball to lay aside all business and try a change of climate for the summer. He would not then relinquish his duties of county treasurer, but after his prostration in July he closed up all of his business affairs here and went to Bristow house in the state of New York, where he died in September 1875. I was with him when he started on his visit to New York but never saw him afterward.

In my opinion, and in which I have no doubts, Col John Ball died from Consumption. The disease originated from his severe duties, hardships and exposure while in the army during the War of the Rebellion. I have no interest directly or indirectly in this affidavit for a pension.

James M. Cole, January 28, 1891, Winona County, Minnesota

FIRST MINNESOTA TIMELINE

1861

April 27, 1861—Fort Snelling, Minn. Ten companies report for duty.

June 26—First Minnesota Infantry arrives in Washington, D.C.

July 21—Battle of Bull Run. The regiment supports Rickett's Battery in an attack on Henry House Hill led by Cos. A and F. Rickett's Battery is lost and recaptured repeatedly until falling to the rebels. Lieutenant Colonel Miller orders retreat.

Aug. 16—Move to Camp Stone near Edwards Ferry.

Oct. 21-22—Battle of Ball's Bluff (Goose Creek). The First Minnesota is removed from the main fighting and only lightly engages.

1862

Feb. 26, 1862—Move to camp at Harper's Ferry.

March 27—Move to the Peninsula. Tents are left behind and finally arrive April 1.

April 5-May 4—Siege of Yorktown. Continual rain without tents.

May 6—Move to West Point, Virginia.

May 25—Set up camp near Chickahominy River, where they build a grape-vine bridge.

May 31-June—Battle of Fair Oaks. The First Minnesota is sent in as reinforcements, where companies H, K, and D engage with the extreme left of the rebels.

June—Set up camp near Fair Oaks (Camp Sully).

June 29—Battle of Savage Station. Defend the left flank. George Burgess, color sergeant, is killed.

June 30—Battle of White Oak Swamp (Glendale). The regiment then marches on to Brackett's Ford and Glendale, where they fight until midnight.

July 2-Aug. 4—Set up camp at Harrison's Landing. President Lincoln visits on July 9.

Aug. 25-28—Move to Alexandria.

Aug. 28-Sept. 2—Hard march under fire to cover the Union retreat at Second Bull Run.

Sept. 17—Battle of Antietam. Exposure to heavy fire from both flanks as the 435-man regiment is on the extreme right of Gorman's brigade as Sedgwick's division. First Minnesota suffers 15 killed, 79 wounded, and 21 missing. They remain camped among the dead on the field.

Sept. 22—Move to Bolivar Heights overlooking Harper's Ferry.

Oct. 30—Move to Stafford Hills near Falmouth.

Dec. 11-15—Battle of Fredericksburg. Capture Fredericksburg and plunder through the night.

1863

Dec. 16-June 15, 1863—Winter quarters near Falmouth.

May 3-5—Battle of Chancellorsville. The First Minnesota misses the main battle but crosses the Rappahannock River into Fredericksburg, where they undergo fire.

June 15-20—Hard march through heat to Uniontown, Pennsylvania.

June 29—Colonel Colvill is arrested for allowing the soldiers to cross a river on logs but is released the following day. The regiment is exhausted upon reaching Gettysburg after marching 14 miles a days over 14 days.

July 2—Battle of Gettysburg. The oncoming Confederates penetrate Sickles's line. Gen. Winfield S. Hancock orders the First Minnesota to charge, delays the rebels, and fills the gap in the line until reinforcements arrive.

July 3—Pickett's charge, shored up by companies C and F, adds another 45 casualties to the first Minnesota losses for a total of 224 at Gettysburg, or 82 percent of the regiment. Medals of Honor are presented to Union

Pvt. Marshall Sherman and Cpl. Henry O'Brien for capturing Confederate colors.

July 24—Battle of Kelly's Farm.

Aug. 15-Sept.6—Stationed in New York City to maintain order after the draft riots.

Oct. 14—Battle of Bristoe Station. Deployed as skirmishers to attack Confederate entrenchments. The attack is called off, but hundreds of Confederates are arrested.

Dec.-Feb. 1864—Winter camp near Culpepper Courthouse.

1864

Feb. 6, 1864—First Minnesota is honored at a banquet at the National Hotel in Washington, D.C. They depart for home the following day.

Feb. 15—St. Paul holds a welcome home reception and 30 furloughs are provided.

April 28—Parade at Fort Snelling. The First Minnesota ranked 23rd out of 2,047 Union regiments in percentage of total enrollment killed. They captured 840 Confederates and two flags, but never lost one of their own colors. Some 58 men re-enlisted with the Union Army to fight in the final campaigns in the East.

1865

During the Reconstruction Era from 1865 to 1867, Union regiments were posted in the key state of Tennessee to maintain control during the transition, introduce new laws, and rebuild the South. John Ball was posted in Gallatin as the lieutenant colonel in command.

Jan. 12, 1865—Tennessee General Assembly prohibits slavery through an amendment to the state constitution.

Feb. 22—Public referendum ratifies an amendment to the state constitution abolishing slavery.

April 3—Occupation of Richmond by Union troops.

April 9—Surrender of Gen. Robert E. Lee to Ulysses S. Grant at Appomattox Court House in Virginia.

April 14—Lincoln is shot by John Wilkes Booth at Ford's Theatre and dies several days later.

April 26—Negotiations take place in North Carolina between Confederate Gen. Joseph Johnston and Gen. William T. Sherman in relation to the surrender of the Army of Tennessee and all other Confederate forces (about 90,000 soldiers). The two leaders become friends for life after Sherman provides 10 days of rations to Johnston's hungry troops. Johnston becomes Sherman's pallbearer upon his death in 1891. With the surrender of Lee's and Johnston's armies, the Civil War ends.

May 29—President Andrew Johnson issues his Amnesty Proclamation. This Reconstruction plan disenfranchises Confederate military leaders and large land owners pending approval of amnesty petitions. All states are ordered to ratify the 13th Amendment, and succession must be declared null and void. The southern state conventions and leadership resist his proclamation.

December—The 13th Amendment is ratified; slavery is officially abolished in the US.

SIGNIFICANT EVENTS
IN THE LIFE OF JOHN BALL

"Nearly all men can withstand adversity;
if you want to test a man's character, give him power."
—*Abraham Lincoln*

Born December 5, 1835: Adopted into the Ball family shortly thereafter.
April 29, 1861: One of the first to enlist as a Union soldier—leaves his job as county surveyor to become orderly sergeant in Co. K of the First Minnesota at age 25, the first state regiment to respond to Lincoln's call.
July 21, 1861: Bull Run—First Minnesota is one of the last regiments to leave the battlefield and suffers the highest casualties of any northern regiment.
Nov 14, 1861: Discharged as an enlisted man and commissioned 2nd lieutenant of the company.
March 9, 1862: Officer of Picket Guard at Charlestown.
March 15, 1862: Marches to Bolivar Heights in rain and sleet.
March 30, 1862: Marches to Alexandria and embarks onboard the Jenny Lind "amid snow and cold."
April 16, 1862: Writes letter from Fortress Monroe Hospital, where he is recovering from what appears to be bronchitis but is the beginning of tuberculosis.
June 27, 1862: Fights in swamps of Chickahominy.
Aug. 28, 1862: Fights at Second Battle of Bull Run.
Sept. 1862: Transfers to Co. F (in Redwing, Minn.).

Sept. 16, 1862: Fights at Antietam.

Sept. 25, 1862: Rear guard on the Peninsula.

Dec. 11-15, 1862: Fights at Fredericksburg.

April 27, 1863: Fights "in the hottest of the fights at Chancellorsville" under Hooker.

May 8, 1863: Camp Falmouth Station, north side of the Rappahannock—takes possession of Fredericksburg.

June 17, 1863: On the March to Gettysburg.

July 2, 1863: Company F detaches as skirmishers at the base of Little Round Top; astronomical losses for the rest of the First Minnesota regiment.

July 3, 1863: Pickett's Charge.

July 6, 1863: Transfers to Company B, where he becomes captain.

Sept. 16, 1863: Fights at Culpeper and the next day skirmishes with the enemy and drives them beyond the Rapidan River.

Oct. 14, 1863: Severely wounded at the Battle of Bristow Station.

Jan. 19, 1864: Returns to duty.

May 5, 1864: Discharged.

Sept. 7, 1864: Accepts commission as lieutenant colonel in command of the 11th Minnesota Volunteer Infantry at the age of 29. Has a regiment in Gallatin, Tennessee.

June 26, 1865: Musters out of the army.

Dec. 27, 1865: Marries Emma C. Lewton in Winona County. They have three children.

1866: Elected representative to the state legislature. Later serves as Winona County Treasurer.

Sept. 26, 1875: Dies in Rutland, New York, at the age of 39.

RESOURCES

The Battle of Gettysburg, as seen by Minnesota Soldiers, Anne A. Hage, June 1963. Minnesota History Magazine. Minnesota Historical Society Press.

Battle of Nashville Preservation Society, Inc., Minnesota regiments at Nashville, *www.bonps.org/features/minnesota-regiments-at-nashville/*.

Child's Gazetteer of Jefferson County, Town of Rutland, New York. 1890.

Editing Historical Documents: A Handbook of Practice, Michael E. Stevens and Steven B. Burg. AltaMira Press/Sage Publications. 1997.

1st Minnesota Volunteer Infantry Regiment, John Ball, Etc. *www.firstminnesota.net/1st.php?ID=0753*.

History of Wabasha County, 1884: Biographical Matter, Statistics, Etc., H. H. Hill and Co. Publishers, Chicago.

Jefferson County History Network, *http://www.usgennet.org/usa/ny/county/jefferson/county.html*.

Jefferson County Journal, Sept. 29, 1875.

Jefferson County, New York, Genealogical Website, Nancy Dixon, *www.jefferson.nygenweb.net/*.

Last Full Measure: The Life and Death of the First Minnesota Volunteers, Richard Moe. Minnesota Historical Society Press. 1994.

Laying the Foundation, *www.Winonahistory.org.*

Minnesota Historical Society Collections, Vol XIV, 1912, MHS, p. 31.

National Archives, pension records, John Ball.

National Park Service, U.S. Dept. of the Interior, *www.civilwartraveler.com/maps/nps/Antietam-park.pdf.*

No More Gallant a Deed: A Civil War Memoir of the First Minnesota Volunteers, James A. Wright and Steven J. Keillor. Minnesota Historical Society Press. 2001.

Pale Horse at Plum Run: The First Minnesota at Gettysburg, Brian Leehan. Minnesota Historical Society Press. 2002.

Portrait and Biographical Record of Winona County, Minnesota, Chicago: Chapman Publishing Company. 1895.

Sick from Freedom: African-American Illness and Suffering During the Civil War and Reconstruction, by Jim Downs, Oxford University Press. 2012.

Tennessee Sesquicentennial Civil War Timeline, compiled by Kraig McNutt, The Center for the Study of the American Civil War, *www.TennesseeintheCivilWar.com.*

Tennessee State Library and Archives, Civil War Research Sources, Tennessee Secretary of State, *www.tennessee.gov/tsla/educationoutreach/Civil War Resources/Timelines/1865 Timeline.doc.*

Winona Daily Republican, multiple articles from 1861-1880.

Made in the USA
Charleston, SC
24 May 2013